D0146582

Islam, Crime and Criminal Justice

Islam, Crime and Criminal Justice

Edited by Basia Spalek

WILLAN
PUBLISHING

Published by

Willan Publishing
Culmcott House
Mill Street, Uffculme
Cullompton, Devon
EX15 3AT, UK
Tel: +44(0)1884 840337
Fax: +44(0)1884 840251
e-mail: info@willanpublishing.co.uk
website: www.willanpublishing.co.uk

Published simultaneously in the USA and Canada by

Willan Publishing
c/o ISBS, 5824 N.E. Hassalo St,
Portland, Oregon 97213-3644, USA
Tel: +001(0)503 287 3093
Fax: +001(0)503 280 8832
e-mail: info@isbs.com
website: www.isbs.com

First published 2002

ISBN 1-903240-89-1 Hardback

British Library Cataloguing-in-Publication Data
A catalogue record for this book is available from the British Library

Printed by T.J. International, Padstow, Cornwall
Typeset by GCS, Leighton Buzzard, Beds.

Contents

Tables

Acknowledgements

I would like to thank David Wilson for suggesting that I edit a book on Islam and the criminal justice system. I am also grateful to all the contributors – Marie Macey, Douglas Sharp, David Wilson, Salah el-Hassan and Natassja Smiljanic – without whom this book would not be possible. In particular, I would like to thank Assma Bibi, Nazira Nathalia and Sadaf Ilyas for their help in developing my understanding of Islam, also the IQRA trust for their support.

Basia Spalek
Birmingham University

Notes on contributors

Salah el-Hassan was born in Khartoum, Sudan. He studied politics at Cairo and London Universities and Criminology in Birmingham. He is the Director of the IQRA Trust Prisoners Welfare and the General Secretary of the National Council for the Welfare of Muslim Prisoners.

Marie Macey (BA, M Ed, PhD, FRSA) is a senior lecturer in sociology. She has published fairly extensively on race/ethnicity and racism in Britain and wider Europe. She is particularly interested in intersections between ethnicity and gender and the role of religion in influencing gendered ethnic and inter-ethnic relations. She is also the Deputy Chair of the Management Committee of the Domestic Violence Agency that ran the first national conference on violence in Asian communities and which also works extensively with Asian women.

Douglas Sharp served for 30 years in the Police Service before taking up his present post as Senior Lecturer in Criminal Justice and Course Director of the BA in criminal justice and policing at the University of Central England in 1995. He is editor of the journal *Police Research and Management* and is a member of the Editorial Advisory Board of *The Howard Journal of Criminal Justice*. He has published work on policing, private security and vigilantism and on the role of Muslims in the criminal justice system.

Natassja Smiljanic is a lecturer in law at the Law School at the University of Central England, Birmingham. Her research interests include international and domestic human rights, war crimes, Islam and human rights and feminist legal theory.

Basia Spalek is a lecturer in community justice studies at Birmingham University. She has published research on victimisation, white-collar crime and race/ethnicity in journals such as the *International Review of Victimology*, the *International Journal of the Sociology of Law* and *The Howard Journal of Criminal Justice*.

David Wilson is Professor of Criminal Justice at the University of Central England in Birmingham. He has researched widely on prisons and the consequences of imprisonment. His most recent books include *Prison (er) Education – Stories of Change and Transformation* (Waterside Press) and *What Everyone in Britain should Know about the Police* (Blackstone Press). He is the Editor of *The Howard Journal of Criminal Justice*.

Chapter 1

Religious diversity, British Muslims, crime and victimisation

Basia Spalek

Introduction

National and international events periodically arise which generate significant media and political interest in the lives of British Muslims because they bring into sharp focus important cultural and religious differences between Muslim communities and wider, 'mainstream' British society. Most recently, the terrorist attacks in America on 11 September 2001, and the subsequent backlash against Muslim communities in the western world, spawned an array of articles and programmes about Islam as it is practised in Britain. Prior to this, the Bradford disturbances that took place in June 1995 and then later between April and July 2001, which involved (amongst others) Muslim Pakistani youths, also placed British Muslims in the public eye, as did the Salman Rushdie affair in 1989. Whilst the contents of this book have been influenced by the recent attacks on the World Trade Center, the book itself was developed as a response to a perceived need to address the issue of religious diversity and to produce a criminological textbook which specifically focuses upon the Islamic faith. There are over one million Muslims living in Britain and to a significant proportion of these individuals Islam is a central part of their lives. As a result, it was considered to be important to put together a collection of pieces which focus on the lives of some Muslims and which document their experiences of crime and criminal justice.

Criminology: a 'modern' discipline that has often bypassed the issue of religion

Within criminological textbooks and research studies, diversity and difference have often been viewed in terms of race or ethnic identity, thereby largely omitting the issue of religious diversity. Using generic labels such as 'Black', 'Asian' and 'ethnic minority' much research has been carried out examining how experiences of crime and criminal justice may differ (Smith 1977; Hudson 1989; Fitzgerald 1993; Burnett and Farrell 1994; Holdaway and Barron 1997; Kalunta-Crumpton 1998; Kershaw *et al* 2000). This work has undoubtedly produced many important results, such as the finding that Black people are more likely to be stopped and searched by the police than 'white' people are; and that they are also more likely to be remanded in custody than released on bail and are over-represented amongst the prison population (Willis 1983; Hood 1992; Smith 1997). Asian groups and other ethnic minorities are more likely to be victims of crime than 'whites'; and fear of crime is greater amongst Asian groups than amongst 'whites' (Fitzgerald and Hale 1996).[1] These sorts of findings have caused researchers to seek explanations for the disparities, which include racial discrimination within, and unequal treatment by, the criminal justice system (Hood 1992; Kalunta-Crumpton 1998), and also socioeconomic deprivation, the age structure of particular minority groups and racist stereotyping (Jefferson 1993; Kalunta-Crumpton 1998).

In classifying people in terms of ethnic identity, one aspect of difference that is largely omitted is that of religious affiliation, which may play a central role in some individuals' lives. It seems that the issue of religion has rarely featured in criminological work. This may partly be attributed to the modern roots of the academic discipline of criminology, which means that values adhered to under modernity have also underpinned much criminological work (Garland 1994). Progress and scientific rationale are two key characteristics of modernity (Smart 1992; Douglas 1994) and these are clearly evident in the study of crime: 'Criminology claims the status of the rational and scientific attempt to study the phenomena of crime. It was born with the death of God. It was meant to aid in the journey, the construction of a secure modernity' (Morrison 1995: 5). As a result, the issue of religion and people's beliefs has rarely featured as an object of study. Whilst historical accounts regarding the influence of evangelical Protestantism on the penal system can be found, little attention has been directed towards the issue of religion in modern prisons (Beckford and Gilliat 1998).[2] Yet the religious affiliation of individuals may in some cases be particularly salient, as in the example of 'Asian' prisoners, almost 60 per cent of whom were classified as Muslim in the

1991 National Prison Survey (Fitzgerald 1993: 32). National and local crime surveys tend to classify people according to their ethnic identities rather than their religious affiliations. The British Crime Survey, for example, has traditionally classified people as belonging to Black (Black-African, Black-Caribbean, Black-Other), Indian, Pakistani or Bangladeshi ethnic identities, thereby largely ignoring commonalities of experience of individuals who follow the same faith. The 1994 National Survey of Ethnic Minorities reveals that when respondents were asked to indicate which two out of twelve elements of self-description were most important to them, the majority of south Asians indicated these to be religion and nationality, with religion being as important or more important than nationality (Modood *et al* 1997: 294). These findings indicate that religion is a central part of self-identity to many south Asians and as such should be a focus of research when studying crime-related issues.

Anti-racist movements and the neglect of religious diversity

The dearth of criminological work looking at religious diversity and how this might influence experiences of crime and criminal justice reflects the approaches taken by government bodies, agencies of the criminal justice system and social service departments. Although the issue of race or ethnic identity has received much attention by policy-makers, religion has tended to be largely ignored, or debated only as a secondary issue. This is partly because most race equality organisations are secular, not religious, and so they are often insensitive to religion-based harassment and abuse. Both social welfare and criminal justice policy anti-discriminatory approaches are largely based on anti-racist models, thereby significantly diminishing the importance of religious issues (Sheriff 2001). Many people who have wanted to make formal allegations of discrimination have therefore had to resort to discrimination on the grounds of race or gender even though they believe that the religion that they follow has been the real reason for their inappropriate treatment (Weller *et al* 2001). As a result, people from a variety of different faiths have criticised secular-based anti-racism responses, including Sikhs, Hindus, Catholics and Jewish people.

British Muslims in particular have criticised the Crime and Disorder Act 1998, which introduced higher penalties for offences that are racially aggravated. Whilst the maximum sentence for common assault is six months and/or a £5,000 fine, the maximum for racially aggravated common assault is two years and/or an unlimited fine. A 'racial group' is, for the purposes of the Act (S. 28(4)), 'a group of persons defined by reference to race, colour, nationality or ethnic or national origins'. This is the same definition as used in the Race Relations Act 1976. This does not include religious groups, although Jews and Sikhs are covered as a result of case law. According to police guidelines, it is important to investigate whether an offence, which may appear to be motivated by religious hostility, also contains racial hostility because in this way an attack on a Muslim might be classified as racially aggravated. A number of police forces have also included a reference to religion in their definition of hate crime and are taking into consideration if a racist offence has occurred in a religious building when recording crime. However, these approaches have been criticised by Muslim groups for their perceived inability to deal with anti-Muslim hate crime sufficiently. It has been argued that a possible consequence is that attacks on Jews and Sikhs will be punished more severely than assaults against persons who follow a different religion. Thus, a Muslim youth who punches a Sikh youth may be classed as a racially aggravated assault, yet a Sikh youth punching a Muslim youth may be classed as only common assault (Addison and Lawson-Cruttenden 1998). Guidelines drawn up for statutory, voluntary and community groups in response to the Stephen Lawrence inquiry report have also been criticised by Muslim groups, for what is perceived as being an anti-racist movement that fails to address hate crimes against religious communities. It seems that Muslims have become disillusioned with an anti-racism movement that refuses to combat Islamophobia (Commission on the Future of Multi-Ethnic Britain 2000).

Victim services can be accused of failing to address the religious and spiritual needs of some victims. It appears that religious identity has largely been ignored, and programmes have instead attempted to accommodate racial rather than religious diversity. Religion may in some cases be a better way of understanding people than purely through the framework of race. For example, it may be the case that the needs of south Asian Muslim women may not be the same as the needs of Asian Sikh and Hindu women, but rather may be more similar to English, Bosnian or Arab Muslim women (Sheriff 2001). As a result, incorporating an appreciation of religion within victim frameworks would perhaps mean that a more sensitive approach to victimisation could be developed, one that acknowledges the specific practical and spiritual needs of victims.

Although it might be argued that Britain is a multicultural and multi-faith society, with only 10 per cent of people attending Anglican churches, it might still be considered to be a Christian country. The Queen is the supreme governor of the Church of England, the Church has bishops in the House of Lords and tends to have access to government ministers on important issues. The Christian religion is also taught in many schools, although alongside other faiths (Ward 1992). The Church of England has many privileges as a result of being the most representative religious organisation in England and also as a result of it representing the state (Beckford and Gilliat 1998). This means that Christianity, in particular the Church of England, occupies a privileged role in the criminal justice system, thereby having the effect of marginalising other faiths. For example, within the penal system, Christianity is the dominant religious force, as evidenced by the Prison Act 1952 which requires that every prison has a chaplain who should be Church of England (ibid).

There are some indications that policy-makers have recently started to take notice of the issue of religious discrimination and harassment. A Home Office report was published in 2001, entitled *Religious Discrimination in England and Wales* (Weller *et al* 2001). This report found that whilst in theory it is difficult to disentangle discrimination based on religious grounds from discrimination based on ethnicity, in practice some of the persons who were questioned in this study did appear to be the targets of discrimination and violence as a result of their religious beliefs and practices (ibid.). Controversy recently erupted in the autumn of 2001 when the emergency anti-terror bill the British government had put together in the wake of the terrorist attacks in America included a ban on incitement to religious hatred, in response to the backlash against British Muslim communities. Critics argued that this would stifle free speech and legitimate debate amongst different religious groups. The Home Secretary, David Blunkett, countered these claims by insisting that prosecutions would only take place if they were considered to be in the public interest and cases would only succeed if it could be proved that there was an 'intention' and a 'likelihood' that the use of threatening, abusive or insulting words would arouse hatred. Nonetheless, the government was unable to defeat its opposition and was forced to drop the ban on incitement of religious hatred from the anti-terror bill in order to secure the successful passage of the bill through Parliament. This was despite the fact that Muslim communities have for a long time campaigned for protection against anti-religious discrimination and violence, believing that a law against incitement to religious hatred could close legal loopholes that far-right groups such as the National Front and British National Party have been exploiting.

The rationale for this book

Insensitivity to religious issues can be criticised on the basis that important aspects of crime and victimisation are largely bypassed. People are viewed predominantly from an ethnic perspective, yet ethnicity does not always correspond with religious identity. Moreover, through focusing upon ethnicity, important questions are not addressed. It may be the case, for example, that the ways in which a particular religion is interpreted may lead a person to commit particular types of crime. Religion may significantly influence perceptions and experiences of crime and criminal justice and, as such, should be carefully considered by policy-makers and criminal justice and voluntary agencies when responding to both the perpetrators and victims of crime. For people who work for the criminal justice system, as prison officers, police officers, probation officers and so forth, their religious beliefs may also influence their working practices or may act as a point of discrimination and abuse. This book examines one marginalised, yet popular, religion and generates questions about how following the Islamic faith influences people's experiences of crime and the criminal justice system.

Heterogeneity amongst the British Muslim population

Using the term 'Islam' in this book is in itself rather problematic and misleading as it gives the impression there is one community of Muslim people who have very similar beliefs and practices. However, individuals classified as being Muslim in the UK are heterogeneous, as they originally came from different countries, speak different languages and follow different schools of Islamic thought (Joly 1995). Using the term 'Islam' is also problematic in terms of the negative stereotypes often associated with this religion. Said (1981: xv) has argued that 'Islam' has often been linked to barbarism, medieval theocracy or a kind of distasteful exoticism in western academic, political and social discourses. The term 'Islam' is used in this book, not so as to reproduce these dominant, misleading understandings, but rather to stress the commonalities of experience of British Muslims with respect to criminal justice issues. To a significant proportion of these persons, religion occupies a central role in their lives. The 1994 National Survey of Ethnic Minorities revealed that 90 per cent of Muslims surveyed considered religion to be important to the way they lead their lives, with a substantial majority attending mosque at least once a week (although nearly a third of women do not attend mosque or prayer meetings as this is not an important requirement as it is for men) (Modood *et al* 1997: 302). Hence it is of paramount importance that aspects of crime and criminal justice are addressed in terms of how they are experienced by Muslims.

All the available statistics on the number of Muslims living in Britain are only estimates, since the General Census has not traditionally included questions about religious affiliation. The 1991 General Census includes ethnic and national categories, which is one way in which researchers have estimated the number of people following a particular faith. However, this approach is rather problematic since all the individuals belonging to a specific category do not necessarily follow the same religion. For example, not all Bangladeshis are Muslims, some are Hindu; some Pakistanis are also Christian (Lewis 1994). This means that other surveys have often been used in order to back up data generated from the General Census. For example, the Office of Population Censuses and Surveys (OPCS) and national surveys of ethnic minorities carried out by the Policy Studies Institute have also been used (Lewis 1994; Joly 1995).

The 2001 census in England and Wales has, for the first time, asked individuals to classify themselves according to the following categories: Christian, Buddhist, Hindu, Jewish, Muslim, Sikh or None. However, as the results of this census will not be available until approximately the middle of 2003 (Census Dissemination Unit 2001), for the purposes of this book we must use previous estimates of the Muslim population. In general, there are considered to be approximately one million Muslims in Britain (although some authors have argued that the total amount is more than this) (Lewis 1994: 14; Nielsen 1992 in Joly 1995: xi). Approximately one-third of these are of Pakistani origin; 100,000 come from east Africa; at least 80,000 are from India; and over 60,000 from Bangladesh. The rest have Arabic, Iranian, Turkish, Malaysian and Nigerian origins (Joly 1995: xii). Islam is not only a culturally and ethnically diverse religion, but also is spiritually diverse. There are two main strands to Islam – Shi'a and Sunni. Some 90 per cent of Muslims worldwide are Sunni Muslims, and this percentage is even greater for south Asian Muslims in Britain. Within the Sunni tradition, there are a number of different movements, including Barelwis, Deobandis, Tablighi Jamat and Jama'at-I-Islami (Conway 1997). Of course, religious practices also change and evolve over time (Khan 1999).

Muslim offenders: social exclusion, Islamophobia and interpretations of Islam

Statistics are available regarding the number of individuals classified as Muslim who are imprisoned. According to the Prison Statistics England and Wales (2000), there were 4445 Muslims, 418 Sikh, 254 Hindu male and female prisoners on 30 June. Spalek and Wilson's chapter (Chapter 5) looks more closely at the issue of practising Islam in the penal system. Islam is currently the fastest-growing non-Christian religion in British prisons; whilst the number of Muslim prisoners has significantly increased, those registering as Christians has steadily decreased (Beckford and Gilliat 1998). Through interviewing a group of Imams who regularly visit Muslim prisoners, the study reported in this book suggests that anti-Muslim sentiment is a commonplace feature of prison life. A further important issue to address is that of the over-representation of Muslims in the prison population, when taking into account that although there are approximately one million Muslims in Britain, there are an estimated 500,000 Sikhs, 500,000 Hindus and 300,000 Jews (Commission on the Future of Multi-Ethnic Britain 2000). Clearly, it is important to ask some questions about the Muslim population and why it is the case that the number imprisoned is so high. This issue once more highlights the negative consequences on focusing upon ethnic identity to the detriment of religious affiliation. Researchers looking at rates of imprisonment amongst different ethnic groups have found that although individuals classified as Black are over-represented amongst the prison population, those classified as Asian are under-represented (Smith 1997). The question has then been posed as to why, if both ethnic groups experience similar material deprivation and racial discrimination, are so many black people in prison? This kind of reasoning ignores the over-representation of Muslims in prison in comparison to Sikhs and Hindus. Are there social, economic and perhaps some religious factors which might account for the large amount of Muslims in prison? Age may be a factor here because approximately 70 per cent of all British Muslims are under the age of 25 (Conway 1997), and the age at which offending most commonly starts is 14, whilst the age at which it most commonly stops is 23 (Farrington 1997). Social deprivation and discrimination are also important. The link between social deprivation and offending is now well established (ibid.) and would appear to be a factor in offending amongst some young Muslim men. Racial inequality is evident in the labour market. The rate of unemployment of ethnic minority people is at least double the rate of unemployment of white people (ibid.: 112). People from ethnic minority groups are also more likely to work in low-paid jobs with poor conditions of employment than white people (Bloch 1997: 113). It is clear that social exclusion and inequality are high amongst Muslim communities. According to the Labour Force Survey 1994, Pakistani and Bangladeshi communities (the majority of whom are Muslim) tend to be least well paid (ibid.: 114). In Bradford, unemployment is high in Muslim communities and around half of Pakistani and Bangladeshi households have no full-time workers (Ratcliffe 1996). It is in these areas that public disturbances and riots have taken place. It might be argued that the disadvantage experienced by young Muslim men as a result of racist practices and discrimination is further compounded by anti-Muslim sentiment and hostility in Britain. The Islamophobia report found 'Islamophobia' to be endemic in British society, and defined this as follows: 'The term

Islamophobia refers to unfounded hostility towards Islam. It refers also to the practical consequences of such hostility in unfair discrimination against Muslims and to the exclusion of Muslims from mainstream political and social affairs .... Islam is seen as violent and aggressive' (Conway 1997: 10).

It may be the case that extremist Islamist groups, aware of the lack of educational opportunities and high levels of unemployment, attempt to influence disaffected youths (Commission on the Future of Multi-Ethnic Britain 2000). Indeed, extremist organisations have been accused of targeting penal establishments in order to find new recruits for their causes. However, this has been staunchly denied by Muslim groups, who argue that only two organisations have any contact with prisoners. These are the National Council for the Welfare of Muslim Prisoners and the IQRA Trust. Nonetheless, in the wake of the terrorist attacks of 11 September 2001, prison authorities in Britain have become very sensitive to the issue of the expression of fundamentalist viewpoints, and suspended three Imams for allegedly making inappropriate comments about the terrorist attacks to inmates. One was later expelled, the second was reinstated after an investigation had been conducted and the third is currently awaiting the results of an investigation.

The use of religion for violence and terror has featured in both Christian and Muslim religions. With respect to Islam, whilst there are many passages in the Qur'an teaching mercy and forgiveness towards others, there are nonetheless some which may be open to violent interpretation (although this, of course, applies to the Bible) (Sullivan 2001). Cultural and personal interpretations of the Qur'an may be implicated in some criminal offences. These may sometimes, by a minority of individuals, be used as a way of justifying acts of physical violence against women, gay men, lesbians and prostitutes. In some communities, some men have policed women's behaviour and inflicted psychological and physical violence on women who transgress cultural norms and dress codes (Macey 1999). In order to develop an understanding of criminality amongst some individuals in some Muslim communities, it might therefore be argued that it is important to take into account personal and cultural interpretations of Islam. For instance, Marie Macey's chapter in this book (Chapter 2) illustrates how some young Pakistani Muslim men in Bradford have developed a brand of ethnic activism which has been described as aggressive and macho. This can sometimes lead to their involvement in crime and has been linked to the public disturbances in Bradford which recently took place between April and July 2001, and which were identified by the media as the worst case of urban rioting on the British mainland for 20 years. The disturbances are estimated to have cost the city between £7.5 and £10 million (Denham 2001) and the police £10 million. Hundreds of young Muslim men used petrol bombs, stones and baseball bats as weapons and around two hundred police were injured. It seems that material deprivation, unemployment, police mistreatment, racism, Islamophobia and the 'far right' also played some role in the disturbances.

Muslims and victimisation: hate crime, religion as social support and secular responses to victimisation

Victimisation is another area that deserves to be explored from a perspective that acknowledges religious diversity. Although the process of victimisation has been well documented in terms of the psychological, emotional, financial and behavioural costs of crime, little analysis has been carried out regarding the impact of religious beliefs on this process. Spalek's chapter in this book (Chapter 3), which looks at the crime experiences of a group of Muslim women living in Birmingham, illustrates how Islam can be a central source of support for victims, helping them to move more quickly from 'victim' to 'survivor' status. The women featured in this chapter clearly illustrate the many internal and external resources available to them to help them cope with crime and violence. For example, family as well as the local community can sometimes be a great source of comfort, as is prayer and Islamic spiritual guidance. This may mean that external agencies such as Victim Support are not always required. At the same time, state and voluntary responses to victimisation may be criticised on the basis of their insensitivity to religious need. Secular women's refuges, for example, often provide inadequate support and so many Muslim women choose to remain in their abusive domestic environments (Sheriff 2001). As a response to this, the Muslim Women's Helpline was established in 1990 in order to act as an emotional support to Muslim women for a wide range of issues including divorce, domestic violence, arranged marriages, sexual abuse and incest. However, it has not as yet received any funding from the government and relies upon voluntary donations.

Religion can also be a target for hate crime, particularly when individuals who follow a particular faith are visibly different. In this respect, the events that occurred in the USA on 11 September 2001, when terrorists linked to the extremist Islamist group al-Qaida destroyed the twin towers that comprised the World Trade Center, are particularly salient and have had a significant impact on the way in which this book has developed. Anti-Muslim sentiment and Islamophobia, which have been a long-standing feature within western societies, were heightened in the aftermath of the atrocities that were committed.[3] Muslim men, women and children, as well as places of worship, became the targets of hate crime. Violent attacks on Muslims became more common. For instance, in Manchester a woman was attacked with a hammer, and the assailant is reported to have shouted: 'You should die. You want killing for what you did in America' (*Guardian* 29 September 2001). Other Muslim women have had their head scarves pulled off their heads, have been shouted at and had various attacks committed against their homes (Islamic Human Rights Commission 2001). Graffiti and emails have been sent to individuals with messages such as 'You don't belong here, you never will' (*The Independent* 1 October 2001). Mosques have also repeatedly been attacked. In Bolton in the days that followed the terrorist attacks in New York, a mosque was firebombed (ibid.). In America also Muslim and Sikh communities were targeted. Two men were murdered: one was a Pakistani Muslim and the other an Indian Sikh in acts which were described as revenge killings after the terror attacks (*The Independent* 17 September 2001). As a result, Muslim communities across the western world have been living in a state of heightened anxiety, as evidenced by their requests for greater police protection and their precautionary strategies to try to avoid becoming the targets of hate crime. These might include putting up signs outside mosques which condemn the terrorist attacks in America, and Muslim women in Britain have been issued with a set of guidelines to try to reduce the likelihood of them being attacked (Siddiqui 2001). This discussion clearly illustrates the importance of introducing the issue of religious identity into the debate on fear of crime. Ethnic identity rather than religious affiliation has been the traditional way of classifying individuals, and this has meant that, for Indian, Pakistani or Bangladeshi people, their fear of crime has often been documented according to the general category of 'Asian'. Religious harassment, and its potential, as one important dimension to crime-related anxiety, has therefore largely remained undocumented, yet may be particularly salient in some people's lives. Similarly, the ways in which fear of crime is managed by particular religious communities has not been explored. Spalek's study (Chapter 3) illustrates that, for some Muslim women, the veil is an important aspect to their management of male sexuality, and therefore is an important dimension to their management of fear of potential violence from men.

Researching Islam: ethical dilemmas and barriers to research

Clearly, criminological work has much to gain from an increased focus upon religious diversity. A lack of Muslim criminologists has no doubt contributed to the neglect of research here. The majority of the contributors to this book are 'white' 'non-Muslims' and this then raises the issue of the appropriateness of non-Muslims carrying out this kind of work. Certainly, negative stereotyping of Muslims and gross misunderstandings and representations of Islam have been pervasive in western political and social arenas. Islam has often been interpreted as 'the other', as the antithesis of western society. The West has often defined itself against Islam, with Islam being portrayed as inhumane, barbaric and evil. Islam has often been viewed in monolithic ways, as an unchanging religion which lacks cultural diversity (Said 1978). Islamic law has often been presented as incomplete and inadequate in comparison to 'modern' European law. Islamic law has therefore been delegitimised whilst European law has been viewed as complete and established (Strawson 1993). White, non-Muslim social commentators and journalists have played a significant role in propagating these false impressions of Islam. Recently, for example, *The Independent* published an article called 'In defence of Islamophobia' which again generated stereotypes of Muslim women as being oppressed and under the control of violent men (Islamic Human Rights Commission 2001). In the aftermath of the attacks on 11 September 2001, Mr Berlusconi, the Italian Prime Minister, claimed that western civilisation was superior because of its respect for human rights. These remarks were widely condemned, forcing Mr Berlusconi to apologise as well as argue that his comments had been taken out of context (*The Independent* 17 September 2001). Strawson (1993) questions the way in which western countries have portrayed themselves as being democratic and promoting human rights as opposed to 'defective' Islamic societies which need to be 'fixed'. In his words (ibid.):

> How can Europeans claim this superiority, particularly in the fields of human rights, democracy and pluralism, when our entire societies have been founded on the systematic denial of these benefits to the population of the colonised world until well into the second half of this century? The European systems of law have been used to imprison many who fought for these principles in the colonial world. The European age of the Enlightenment produced the American constitution that permitted slavery, and confined the vote to white male property-holders of the Christian religion.

Claims to moral, legal and political superiority, and the abusive portrayal of Islam by the West, must form a cautionary backdrop to any text written by western non-Muslim academics. Gaining the trust and standpoints of Muslims must be the primary aim, alongside adopting a critical stance towards mechanisms and processes that serve to reproduce dominant misrepresentations of Islam. In the same way that Gelsthorpe (1993) argues that 'white' researchers can study 'black' people, I would suggest that non-Muslims can carry out research on Islam. But this requires active involvement with Muslim organisations and individuals in order to understand and try to portray their worldviews and lifestyles. It also requires the researcher to question his or her own understandings of Islam and the bases of these (mis)understandings. All the researchers who have contributed chapters to this book have striven to develop links with Muslim communities and organisations, and have become actively engaged with issues related to Islam. David Wilson, for instance, has established a close relationship with the IQRA Trust, which is a Muslim educational organisation dedicated to promoting a greater understanding of Islam among Muslims and non-Muslims alike in Britain. The IQRA Prisoners' Welfare group was set up in 1996 with the help of (amongst others) David Wilson. Marie Macey is a social scientist living and working in Bradford. As such her account of male Muslim youth in Bradford is infused with the kinds of details and issues that derive from having a 'lived experience' of the area. Similarly, Basia Spalek's analysis of Muslim women's fear of crime and their experiences of crime emerges from the development of a close working relationship with the women who took part in her study – a significant proportion of the women who were interviewed were students at the same university Basia Spalek worked in. Through getting to know the lives these women were leading, it was possible to gain some understanding of their management of crime-related anxiety.

None the less, there is a desperate need for Muslim researchers to examine criminal justice issues. Non-Muslims cannot directly provide 'insider' accounts of Muslim lives, nor the full extent of the impact and scale of hate crime. Diversity in academic life must be encouraged through the reintroduction of adequate student grants; in this way individuals from socially excluded backgrounds may have a chance to contribute to academic discourse. A deeper problematic that is alluded to in this book is that of the tensions that can arise between the interpretations and values of Islam and the Judeo-Christian values that pervade British society. Islam can provide individuals with particular perspectives and lifestyles which may conflict with the policies adopted by the police, the courts, the prison system and so forth. It is important for us to increase our knowledge of Islamic perspectives and traditions so that a constructive dialogue can take place between Muslim communities and agencies of the criminal justice system. This book makes a small contribution to this debate.

A summary of of the chapters

The main body of this book consists of seven chapters, each of which looks at a separate, but related, aspect of crime and criminal justice in terms of the experiences of British Muslims. The book begins with a contribution from Marie Macey, who examines the criminal activities of young Muslim men living in Bradford. Social exclusion and disadvantage, together with the tensions inherent between their youth subcultures and the traditional patriarchal structures of their families, have sometimes led to their involvement in crime and which can also be implicated in the public disturbances which recently took place in Bradford. Some young men in Bradford have also mobilised a particular form of Islam which has been used aggressively, and sometimes violently, against women. Chapter 3 (by Basia Spalek), focuses upon the fear of crime, and experiences of victimisation, of a group of Muslim women living in Birmingham who wear the Hijab (or veil). The Hijab can have the effect of liberating women from the male (sexual) gaze and, as such, is a central part in the management of crime-related anxiety by these women. At the same time, however, the Hijab can arouse aggression, harassment and hostility from the wider non-Muslim community. This study has found that, particularly after the events of 11 September 2001, Muslim women who veil have been the targets of hate crime. Chapter 4 (written by Douglas Sharp) presents the results of an empirical study commissioned by the IQRA Trust that documents the experiences and attitudes of a group of Muslim police officers. Religion is an important aspect of these officers' lives and can at times conflict with police culture and social activities. This chapter also highlights the need for the Police Service to respond more positively to the cultural and religious diversity of its officers, as there is a distinct lack of Halal food and prayer-room facilities at operational police stations. Chapter 5 is based on a recently published study by Basia Spalek and David Wilson which was featured in *The Howard Journal* (February 2001) entitled 'Not just visitors to prisons: the experiences of Imams who work inside the penal system'. This chapter looks at the penal system and considers the extent to which the spiritual and religious needs of Muslim prisoners have been met. Christianity, in particular the Church of England, has traditionally provided religious care to prisoners and so Chapter 5 looks at the extent to which Islam is marginalised within a penal setting through presenting the results of a study which explored the experiences of a group of Imams who visit Muslim prisoners. Anti-Muslim sentiment and Islamophobia are barriers the Imams have often had to face and overcome. Chapter 6 has been written by Salah el-Hassan, the Director of the IQRA Trust. This is a short chapter which presents a historical account of the IQRA Trust, including its involvement with the HM Prison Service. Chapter 7 (by Natassja Smiljanic), looks at human rights legislation and its impact upon British Muslim communities. Smiljanic demonstrates that the human rights of many Muslims are violated on a daily basis in terms of work, education and personal safety. However, relying upon a primarily legalistic response to redress Muslims' human rights violations, through the adoption of the Human Rights Act 1998, is unlikely to provide Muslims with adequate protection because legalistic interpretations of discrimination are based on race rather than religion. Smiljanic argues that broader cultural, social, political and economic policies must be developed in order to respond more fully to the discrimination and abuse encountered by many Muslims since human rights contain social, cultural and interpersonal dimensions.

Conclusion

This chapter has set out the reasons why it is important to focus upon criminal justice issues in terms of religious rather than ethnic diversity. It has been argued that an approach which seeks to consider aspects of crime and criminal justice through the lens of Muslim identities and experiences would make a significant contribution to a largely forgotten area. Important themes which have been raised here include: the limitations of secular-based responses to discrimination, harassment and violence which often incorporate notions of ethnic rather than religious identity; the dominance of Christianity in the criminal justice system and the subsequent marginalisation of other faiths; the social exclusion and disenfranchisement of young Muslim men and the significance of this when looking at the criminal activity of a proportion of Muslim youth; hate crime against British Muslims, particularly since the events of 11 September 2001; and the tensions that exist between western responses to crime and victimisation and Muslims' lifestyles. These themes feature in the chapters that follow.

Notes

1 The terms 'ethnic minority' and 'Asian' have been criticised. These kinds of labels do not reflect the diversity of the individuals who are classified within their ambit. They also signify the notion of 'otherness' since they carry an array of assumptions about the individuals thus labelled, who are considered to be different from 'white' people (Khan 1999). These terms can be used as a form of

exclusionary power against individuals considered to be 'the other' (Bowling 1998).

2 In response to this, the book *Religion in Prison* (Beckford and Gilliat 1998) was recently published.

3 It is also important to point out, however, that since 11 September, in Bradford attacks by Muslims against other ethnic/religious groups have also increased. The violent attack on a local vicar and his church is one example of this.

References

Addison, N. and Lawson-Cruttenden, T. (1998) *Harassment Law and Practice.* London: Blackstone Press.

Beckford, J. and Gilliat, S. (1998) *Religion in Prison: Equal Rites in a Multi-Faith Society.* Cambridge: Cambridge University Press.

Bloch, A. (1997) Ethnic inequality and social security policy. In A. Walker and C. Walker (eds.) *Britain Divided: The Growth of Social Exclusion in the 1980s and 1990s.* London: CPAG, pp. 111–22.

Bowling, B. (1998) *Violent Racism, Victimisation, Policing and Social Context.* Oxford: Oxford University Press.

Burnett, R. and Farrell, G. (1994) *Reported and Unreported Racial Incidents in Prisons. Occasional Paper* 14. Oxford: Centre for Criminological Research, University of Oxford.

Campbell, D. (2001) San Diego: gripped by the fear factor. *The Guardian* 29 September.

Carrell, S. (2001) Muslim leaders warn of riots over anti-terror law. *The Independent* 11 November.

Carrell, S. and Gumbel, A. (2001) Murders of Asian men in US heighten fears of revenge attacks. *The Independent* 17 September.

Census Dissemination Unit (2001) http://census.ac.uk/cdu/

Commission on the Future of Multi-Ethnic Britain (2000) *The Parekh Report.* London: Profile Books.

Conway, G. (1997) *Islamophobia: A Challenge for Us All.* London: The Runnymede Trust.

Crime and Disorder Act (1998) http://www.hmso.gov.uk/acts/acts1998/19980037.htm

Denham, J. (2001) *Building Cohesive Communities: A Report of the Ministerial Group on Public Disorder and Community Cohesion.* London: HMSO.

Douglas, M. (1994) *Purity and Danger: An Analysis of the Concepts of Pollution and Taboo* London: Routledge & Kegan Paul.

Farrington, D. (1997) Human development and criminal careers. In M. Maguire *et al* (eds.) *The Oxford Handbook of Criminology* (2nd edn). Oxford: Clarendon Press, pp. 361-408.

Fitzgerald, M. (1993) *Ethnic Minorities and the Criminal Justice System.* London: HMSO.

Fitzgerald, M. and Hale, C. (1996) *Ethnic Minorities, Victimisation and Racial*

Harassment. Research Findings 39. London: HMSO.

Garland, D. (1994) Of crimes and criminals: the development of criminology in Britain. In M. Maguire *et al* (eds.) *The Oxford Handbook of Criminology.* Oxford: Oxford University Press, pp. 17–68.

Gelsthorpe, L. (1993) Approaching the topic of racism: transferable research strategies? In D. Cook and B. Hudson (eds.) *Racism and Criminology.* London: Sage, pp. 77–95.

Guardian (2001) Hammer attack on Asian woman. 28 September.

Holdaway, S. and Barron, A. (1997) *Resigners? The Experience of Black and Asian Police Officers.* London: Macmillan.

Hood, R. (1992) *Race and Sentencing.* Oxford: Clarendon Press.

Hudson, B. (1989) Discrimination and disparity: the influence of race on sentencing. *New Community* 16(1): 23–4.

Islamic Human Rights Commission (2001) http://www.ihrc.org/Islamophobia/fact-fiction.htm

Jefferson, T. (1993) The racism of criminalisation: police and the reproduction of the criminal other. In L. Gelsthorpe (ed.) *Minority Ethnic Groups in the Criminal Justice System.* Cambridge: Institute of Criminology, pp. 26–48.

Joly, D. (1995) *Britannia's Crescent: Making a Place for Muslims in British Society.* Aldershot: Avebury.

Kalunta-Crumpton, A. (1998) The prosecution and defence of black defendants in drugs trials. *British Journal of Criminology* 38(4): 561–91.

Kelso, P. (2001) Prison Imam suspended for anti-US stance. *The Guardian* 28 December.

Kershaw, C., Budd, T., Kinshott, G., Mattinson, J., Mayhew, P. and Myhill, A. (2000) *The British Crime Survey 2000. Home Office Statistical Bulletin* 18. London: HMSO.

Khan, S. (1999) *A Glimpse through Purdah: Asian Women – the Myth and the Reality.* Oakhill: Trentham Books.

Lewis, P. (1994) *Islamic Britain: Religion, Politics and Identity among British Muslims.* London: I.B. Tauris & Co.

Macey, M. (1999) Class, gender and religious influences on changing patterns of Pakistani Muslim male violence in Bradford. *Ethnic and Racial Studies* 22(5): 845–66.

Modood, T., Berthoud, R., Lakey, J., Nazroo, J., Smith, P., Virdee, S. and Beishon, S. (1997) *Ethnic Minorities in Britain: Diversity and Disadvantage.* London: Policy Studies Institute.

Morrison, W. (1995) *Theoretical Criminology: From Modernity to Post-modernism.* London: Cavendish.

Prison Statistics England and Wales (2000) London: HMSO.

Ratcliffe, P. (1996) *Race and Housing in Bradford.* Bradford: Bradford Housing Forum/Cambridge: Cambridge University Press.

Said, E. (1978) *Orientalism.* Harmondsworth: Penguin Books.

Said, E. (1981) *Covering Islam: How the Media and the Experts Determine How We See the Rest of the World.* London: Routledge.

Sheriff, S. (2001) Presentation to the Victim Support annual conference, 3 July, University of Warwick.

Siddiqui, S. (2001) The Islamic Human Rights Commission http://www.ihrc.org/file7.htm

Smart, B. (1992) *Modern Conditions, Postmodern Controversies.* London: Routledge.

Smith, D. (1977) *Racial Disadvantage in Britain.* Harmondsworth: Penguin Books.

Smith, D. (1997) Ethnic origins, crime and criminal justice. In M. Maguire *et al* (eds.) *The Oxford Handbook of Criminology* (2nd edn). Oxford: Oxford University Press, pp. 703–60.

Spalek, B. and Wilson, D. (2001) Not just visitors to prisons: the experiences of Imams who work inside the penal system. *The Howard Journal of Criminal Justice* 40(1): 3–13.

Strawson, J. (1993) Encountering Islamic law. Paper presented at the Critical Legal Conference, 9–12 September, New College, Oxford.

Sullivan, A. (2001) This *is* a religious war. *The New York Times Magazine* 7 October.

Vallely, P. (2001) MP tries to allay Muslim fears over 'war on Islam'. *The Independent* 1 October.

Ward, K. (1992) Is a Christian state a contradiction? In D. Cohn-Sherbok and D. McLellan (eds.) *Religion in Public Life.* London: Macmillan, pp. 5–16.

Weller, P., Feldman, A. and Purdam, K. (2001) *Religious Discrimination in England and Wales. Home Office Research Study* 220. London: HMSO.

Willis, C. (1983) *The Use, Effectiveness and Impact of Police Stop and Search Powers. Home Office Research and Planning Unit Paper* 15. London: HMSO.

Chapter 2

Interpreting Islam: young Muslim men's involvement in criminal activity in Bradford

Marie Macey

Introduction

This chapter was written as the majority of the world reeled in horror at the terrorist attack on the USA that is thought to have cost around six thousand North American lives. The economic, social and, perhaps, military consequences of the incident are as yet unknown, but are likely to be far-reaching for all of us. For Muslims they will be worse if evidence corroborates speculation that the attack was carried out by Islamic extremists. In both Britain and America, Muslims have already suffered insults, threats and assaults, echoing the experience of the Irish in Britain following bombings by Irish terrorists (Hickman and Walter 1997).

Writing about Muslim men's involvement in crime at this point in time invites the charge of perpetuating racist and/or religious stereotypes and detracting attention away from the reality of racism in Britain. Even before the attack on America, there was strong pressure on researchers not to publish material that might be seen as critical of minority ethnic groups. Anne Cryer, a Labour Member of Parliament in the Bradford area, was recently vilified for suggesting that lack of competence in English by brides brought to England from the Indian subcontinent could contribute to poverty in the Pakistani community. Rosemary Harris's paper on Bangladeshis in London (Harris 1998), to an Institute for Public Policy research Seminar, resulted in a highly charged debate in which she was criticised for moving too far away from issues of racism and racial discrimination, and it was suggested that a white woman had no right to comment on minority ethnic communities.[1] Criticisms from *within* minority ethnic communities are dismissed as 'inauthentic and westernised' and 'more radical elements of our community are labelled as extremists' (Patel 1998: 22). In Bradford, such labelling is sometimes followed by physical assault, as a number of my students have experienced. Beckett and Macey (2001: 3) refer to '. . . . the development of a "conspiracy of silence" between such diverse groups as minority ethnic men, male academics, professionals and the state', a situation summed up by Afshar's (1994: 144) comment: '. . . . a climate of fear and oppression has been created in this area which extends to research and scholarly pursuits.'

Sir Herman Ousley's investigation into inter-ethnic relations in Bradford describes a city 'in the grip of fear': fear of talking about problems openly; fear of challenging wrong-doing in case of being labelled 'racist'; fear of confronting the gang culture, the illegal drugs trade and the growing racial intolerance, harassment and abuse that exists (Ousley 2001: 1). The Bradford Commission report – an intensive inquiry into the public disorders of 1995 – precedes the Ousley one in pointing to ignorance and fear as major contributors to conflict between ethnic groups.

But fear and oppression and the silencing of voices that suggest alternative analyses of situations do not produce either good social science *or* social policy because the latter is (sometimes) based on the former. Nor do they enhance racialised relations; they may actually worsen them as white people react adversely to constant accusations of racism, observing that 'Asian racism' is ignored or explained away. This is particularly so for those white people who have suffered racially based assaults (as many as 70 per cent of all such assaults in some areas) and who themselves live with deprivation and marginalisation.

I am writing this chapter, then, for two reasons. First, because as both a social scientist *and* a resident of Bradford, I am conscious that much of what is written about ethnic groups and inter-ethnic relations in the city is at best incomplete and at worst inaccurate. Secondly, because I believe that racial equality will only be achieved when we can openly and honestly discuss the difficulties involved in multicultural living for *all* the diverse groups in Britain.[2]

Some conceptual and terminological difficulties

Before an intelligible analysis of young Muslim men's involvement in criminal activity can take place, it is necessary to explain how I am using some key concepts and terms. First, the terms 'Asian' and 'Pakistani' are not strictly correct since the majority of people to whom I refer were born, or mainly brought up, in England and are British citizens. I have retained the terms 1) in the interests of brevity; 2) because official documents and statistics use them and 3) because the people to whom I refer designate themselves in this way, more often referring to Pakistan, not Britain, as 'home'. It should be noted, however, that there are recent indications of change on this dimension as some young Muslims explore a 'British' Muslim identity (Samad 1998).

Secondly, the terms 'Islam' and 'Muslim' are used with caution and in full awareness that they are not homogeneous categories. The variant of Islam adopted by Pakistani men in Bradford is strongly influenced by cultural traditions imported from rural Mirpur, so that what is referred to as an Islamic code is, in many instances, a cultural norm. In addition, *young* Pakistani men have developed a 'Muslim' identity that can be said to owe less to Islamic theology than it does to self-interest (Macey 1999a, 1999b).

Thirdly, the young perpetrators of crime and violence described in this chapter constitute only a tiny percentage of the local Muslim population. However, their behaviour has a disproportionate impact on *all* Bradford residents[3] and is having a negative effect on both inter- and intra-ethnic relations, particularly gendered and generational ones.

Fourthly, public disorder and violence are not restricted to young Pakistani Muslim men in Bradford or elsewhere. Arguably, much of their behaviour has socioeconomic roots, its correlation with ethnicity being largely due to demographic and residency patterns in the areas under discussion. Ethnicity and religion acquire an independent status because 1) the perpetrators of criminal acts use both to legitimate their behaviour; and 2) there are aspects of Islam that can be seen as influencing the potential for crime.

Fifthly, it is important to distinguish between religions and the behaviour that their adherents claim is religiously inspired, for there is often a yawning chasm between the two. Both Christianity and Islam, for example, preach peace, equality and respect for human life, yet both have been – and are – used to legitimise injustice, oppression and warfare (Allen and Macey 1995). Al Sadaawi (1991) comments that 'governments need God and religion to justify oppressive regimes; politicians use religion and authoritarian governments pursue fundamentalist positions for reasons far removed from theological ones'. It may be that Al Sadaawi's observation can be applied to areas such as Bradford where the (male) politics of the mosque influence individuals, groups, communities and local government decision-making (Patel 1998; Beckett and Macey 2001).

Finally, of immediate significance to this chapter is the fact that crime statistics use the aggregate term 'Asian' to include people of Bangladeshi, Indian and Pakistani origins (Home Office 2000a). There are some exceptions to this, such as data on prison populations that differentiate between ethnicity and religion. Even this, however, does not disaggregate the terms 'black', 'white' and 'other non-white', despite the heterogeneity of the populations comprising these categories. Faced with statistics of limited utility, then, one has to reach conclusions using demographic data on ethnicity and geographical residency patterns supported by information from knowledgeable local groups and individuals. This situation is not perfect and some misclassifications may occur.

Before going on to discuss young Muslim men's involvement in crime, it is important to provide information on the populations concerned and the contexts within which they operate.

South Asian migration to Britain

Britain, like many other western European countries, only became significantly multi-ethnic around 50 years ago when post-World War Two restructuring necessitated the recruitment of overseas labour. Even then, ethnocentrism and racism ensured that non-Europeans were recruited reluctantly, when European labour proved insufficient. The overwhelmingly male migrants who came to Britain were viewed as units of labour and it was assumed that they would return to their countries of origin when they were no longer needed. Migrants were discriminated against in the workplace, lived in appalling conditions and suffered ignorance, prejudice and outright racism in society. Because they subscribed to the 'myth of return' (Anwar 1979), they tolerated this with little, or no, complaint, believing they could amass enough money to return to much improved living conditions in their homelands.

The arrival of women and children from the Indian subcontinent in the 1960s and 1970s had a major impact on Pakistani life in Britain. It contributed to the demise of the 'myth of return', ensured the reimposition of *biradari*[4] control over male sexuality and provided an impetus to self-definition on religious, rather than ethnic, grounds (Shaw 1994). Most migration from the Indian subcontinent took the form of 'chain migration': '. . . . the vast majority of migrants arrived not as unconnected individuals, but in cascading chains along increasingly well-worn paths of kinship and friendship' (Ballard 1994: 11). This resulted in extremely unequal Asian settlement across the country, with ten geographical areas (including West Yorkshire in which Bradford is located) accounting for 85 per cent of the total minority ethnic populations of England and Wales (Home Office 2000a). This means that social structures and kin networks in, for instance, rural Mirpur, have a strong influence on social relationships and organisation in, say, urban Bradford. Ballard (1994: 11) observes that south Asian settlements have a parochial character because '. . . . specific and highly localised castes, sects and kinship groups in the sub-continent have given rise to – and are now umbilically linked with – equally tightly structured British-based ethnic colonies'. This has implications for inter- and intra-ethnic relationships, carrying an impetus towards self, rather than social, exclusion as well as the continuous reproduction of Pakistani culture and religion. Shaw (1994) and Ballard (1994) point to the strong rejection of British society by people of Pakistani origin and their deep concern to avoid the corrupting influence of the West, particularly in relation to sexuality, women and gender segregation. Ballard (1994: 8) remarks:

> . . . . minorities have become an integral part of the British social order, and they have done so *on their own terms*. Hence the underlying challenge is simple: how – and how soon – can Britain's white natives learn to live with difference, and to respect the right of their fellow-citizens to organise their lives on their own preferred terms, whatever their historical and geographical origins?

I would argue that Ballard's question oversimplifies the complexity of inter-ethnic relations and ignores the tensions and conflicts whose effects cross ethnic boundaries. To illustrate this, I first describe minority ethnic populations and their location in Bradford before turning to the question of Muslim involvement in crime there.

South Asians in Bradford[5]

According to the 1991 census, just under 6 per cent of the British population comprise 'visible' minorities whose origins are India (840,000), the Caribbean (500,000), Pakistan (477,000) and Bangladesh (163,000) (Ballard and Kalra 1994). However, the unequal settlement noted above means that cities such as Bradford have far larger south Asian populations than the national average. Ratcliffe produces population statistics for Bradford (Table 2.1) that show changes over a ten-year period.

The largest minority ethnic group in Bradford originates from the Mirpur region of Azad (Free) Kashmir in Pakistan – a rural area that is one of the poorest in the country. The status of Kashmir, partly in India and

Table 2.1: Major ethnic groups in Bradford (1981–91)[6]

Ethnic group	1981	1991	Population change	% change
White	401,490	399,860	−1,630	−0.4
Black Caribbean	2,927	3,508	+581	+19.8
Indian	10,375	12,409	+2,034	+19.6
Pakistani	34,116	48,059	+13,943	+40.9
Bangladeshi	2,259	3,877	+1,618	+71.6

Source: Based on Ratcliffe (1996: 3).[7]

partly in Pakistan, is a major political influence on Pakistanis in Bradford. The Bangladeshis, a relatively small group who arrived later than the Pakistanis, come from Sylhet, which is also a poor rural area. They suffer the greatest proportionate levels of stress in Bradford (Allen and Barrett 1996). There is also a small group of Gujaratis whose origins are Indian but who, like the Pakistanis and Bangladeshis, are Muslim. The small number of east African Asians, from Kenya and Uganda, are from middle-class backgrounds, are fluent in English and well educated. The Indian populations (Hindu and Sikh) are estimated at around 6,000 each. Both are dispersed across the Bradford district and both are relatively prosperous, though their internal class differentiation is marked (Ratcliffe 1996).

Despite a shared religion, Bradford Muslims are not homogeneous. They speak a number of different languages/dialects and are divided into several sects (Samad 1991). The Muslim community is mainly concentrated in a narrow geographical area of the city, where it constitutes the overwhelming majority of residents (Lewis 1994). Four formal investigations in Bradford comment on this geographical segregation and its role in inter-ethnic conflict (Allen and Barrett 1996; Cantle 2001; Denham 2001; Ousley 2001).

Bradford is the fourth largest metropolitan settlement in England. Its population is young (23.6 per cent under 16) and growing (+6 per cent by the year 2011). Population change varies by ethnic group with the Pakistani population predicted to *increase* by 71.7 per cent between 1996 and 2011 and the white one predicted to *decrease* by 6 per cent over the same period (City of Bradford Metropolitan District Council [CBMC] 1996b: 1). This is due to the differential age structure of the white and Pakistani populations, the fact that Muslim families tend to be larger than white ones and the phenomenon of 'white flight'. The latter is compounded in Bradford by 'Indian flight' (Singh 1994) as the city is increasingly perceived as a Muslim enclave.

One in five people in Bradford live in areas of multiple deprivation characterised by poverty, unemployment, poor education, overcrowded housing, crime, drug dealing, firearms and prostitution (CBMC 1993, 1998). Unemployment is high in Muslim communities and around half of Pakistani and Bangladeshi households have no full-time workers (Ratcliffe 1996). It is particularly prevalent in the inner city among young Muslims (CBMC 1996a, 1996b) where it can reach as high as 45 per cent (Taj 1996). It is in these areas that the public violence described in this chapter has taken place. Before discussing this in any detail, I will first look at what we know of Muslim crime more generally.

Ethnicity, religion and crime in England and Wales

The problems of interpreting crime statistics in relation to 'race' and ethnicity are many and well rehearsed. They include the use of such undifferentiated categories as 'Asian', 'Black' and 'White'; changes in behaviour defined as criminal, and differential methods of recording between police forces. Fundamentally, too, the extent of racism, including institutionalised racism, throughout the criminal justice system results in differential arrests, court appearances and sentencing – both in terms of custodial sentences and their length (see Barclay and Mhlanga 2000 on differential decisions by the Crown Prosecution Service; Hood 1992 on race and sentencing; Macpherson 1999 on institutionalised racism in the police; Miller *et al* 2000 on stops and searches; Phillips and Brown 1998 on arrests, and Virdee 1995 on racially motivated violence).

Interpreting crime statistics in terms of race/ethnicity, then, must be done with extreme caution. This is particularly the case when religion is used as an additional variable, and my use of prison statistics must be interpreted in light of all the caveats noted above. There are, however, two interesting aspects of the relationship between ethnicity, religion and crime. The first is that whilst the number of British south Asian males in prison has increased from 1.7 to 2.3 per cent over the six-year period 1994–99, the major change is within the Pakistani population. Bangladeshis and Indians have remained relatively constant at around 0.1 per cent and 0.7 per cent respectively, but Pakistanis have increased from 0.9 per cent in 1994 to 1.3 per cent in 1999 (Home Office 2000a: 41). A second point of interest concerns differences in the types of crime for which Asian, black and white people are imprisoned (see Table 2.2).

A number of these figures fly in the face of commonly held stereotypes of ethnic groups. These include the high rate of violent offences committed by Asians relative to, for instance, black people, and the similarity of both

Table 2.2: Prison population of England and Wales by ethnicity and type of crime, (1999, %)

Offence	Asian	Black	White
Violence against the person	24	18	22
Sexual offences	8	7	10
Burglary	6	10	19
Robbery	10	21	11
Theft and handling	7	5	9
Fraud and forgery	7	2	2
Drugs offences	23	28	13

Source: Based on Home Office (2000a: 45).

groups' involvement in drugs. Whatever the explanations for this (and these must include migration stages and the age reached by Asian populations), the offences listed are common to varying degrees across the British population. There are, however, a number of 'specifically Muslim' crimes that are not immediately apparent from the Table 2.2. I will deal with these mainly in relation to Bradford, since I do not have factual information on their incidence elsewhere.

Muslim male criminal activity in Bradford

The only crime statistics dealing with race/ethnicity for West Yorkshire (a considerably larger area than Bradford) concern 'stops and searches', 'racist incidents' and 'composition of the police force' (West Yorkshire Police 2001). This makes it impossible to see whether Muslim crime in Bradford is similar to that at the national level, though some observations are relevant to this chapter. First, whilst violent crime nationally increased by 16.1 per cent, in West Yorkshire it only rose by 5.1 per cent. Secondly, the types of crime (using the categories in Table 2.2) showing the most significant increases in West Yorkshire were 'violence against the person', 'drugs' and 'handling'. In ethnic terms, the only comment that can be made on these statistics with any level of confidence is that the majority of the illegal drug trade in Bradford is controlled by Pakistani Muslims. This may be related to the fact that, other than cannabis, heroin is the most common drug (West Yorkshire Police 2001: 25) and Muslims have ready access to it in Pakistan (Khan 1997).

What I referred to above as 'specifically Muslim crime' in Bradford stems from, centres around, or is influenced by: 1) perceived religious requirements; 2) international Islam and the notion of *Ummah* (the pan-Islamic nation or brotherhood of Muslims); 3) the politics of the Indian subcontinent; and 4) Mirpuri cultural traditions, sometimes masquerading as religious requirements. These influences are not discrete, but intersect and interact; however, the categories are helpful in understanding particular instances of public disorder.

For example, *religious requirements* were used in 1989 to demand the provision of *Halal* meat for Muslim children in Bradford schools; public demonstrations degenerated into violent disorder. The influence of *international Islam* was seen in 1989 when Bradford Muslims publicly demonstrated support for the *fatwa* declared by Ayatolla Khomeni against the author, Salman Rushdie. The demonstrations included a ritual book burning and ended in violent public disorder. The influence of *politics on the Indian subcontinent* is illustrated by the public disorder that marked the 1995 local elections in Bradford. Because both Conservative and Labour candidates were Pakistani, the high levels of public harassment by roving gangs bewildered many onlookers – until they realised that the candidates were from rival clans in Pakistan.[8] Finally, the influence of *traditions imported from Mirpur* is illustrated by gender relations and sexuality in the Pakistani Muslim community. These have been extended to non-Muslims, with serious effects on racialised conflict in Bradford. This issue highlights the tension that exists between local interpretations of Islamic values and the Judeo-Christian ones that are dominant in British society. For this reason I give several examples of criminal and neo-criminal behaviour in Bradford under this heading.

Under the concept of *izzat* (honour), central to Islamic culture, women carry the entire burden of upholding family and community honour (Khanum 1992), and 'appropriate' female dress and behaviour are taken to signify not only their honour, but that of their families and the wider community (Kassam 1997). The result is that in defence of honour, men go to inordinate lengths to monitor the appearance and behaviour of women (referred to as 'guarding' by Afshar 1994 and 'policing' by Alibhai-Brown 1998). Young Muslim men in Bradford spend a considerable amount of time and energy in controlling 'their' women – control that involves them in a spectrum of behaviour from relatively minor nuisance to murder. One example is the persistent (anonymous) telephoning of 'liberal' parents to tell them that their daughters bring disgrace to the community. A common threat in such cases is to 'run families out of Bradford', a threat that Muslim women say is a real one: 'They can do it and everybody knows that.' Another example of relatively minor nuisance is the constant harassment of young Asian (and other) women by gangs of Muslim males who gather in public places and verbally harass women passers-by.[9] More serious is the mental and physical violence inflicted on female family members perceived as breaching Islamic codes of behaviour, particularly in terms of interaction with men and choice of husbands (Afshar 1989; Ali 1992; Macey 1999a; Beckett and Macey 2001). This takes varying forms, from intense pressure and monitoring of activities, through domestic violence, to the use of gangs and 'bounty hunters' to force women who have fled to return home (Keighley Domestic Violence Forum 1998; Patel 1998; Women Against Fundamentalism 1998). Alibhai-Brown (1998) refers to women who 'vanish' and reports that the coroner's office is unwilling to release information on the suspicious deaths of Asian women. Afshar (1994: 133) comments: '. . . . there are many cases of daughters, wives or sisters being beaten to death, burned or grievously harmed by their kin for transgressing'.

The extension to non-Muslims of cultural traditions (defined as Islamic principles) has led to physical assaults on white college and university staff and students. Although some incidents may reflect inter-ethnic antagonism/racism, others cannot be explained in this way. For example, infringement of Islamic dress codes underpinned the harassment and threats to which a white female student was subjected whilst running on the streets. Assaults on, and death threats to, gay people are justified by the Islamic condemnation of homosexuality.

Following the local election described earlier, Muslim men instigated a campaign against the sex trade in which large numbers of Pakistani Muslim youths engaged in harassment and violence. This started as a peaceful, organised protest, but over eight weeks spiralled out of control as roving gangs of youths (some from surrounding areas) violently harassed prostitutes to drive them out of the area. The vigilante activity which characterised the campaign was publicly defined as an 'Islamic cause' – a claim that I noted (Macey 1999a) would have been more convincing if the majority of 'pimps' and 'punters' had not been Pakistani Muslims!

In sum, young Pakistani Muslim men in Bradford have developed a brand of ethnic activism described by Ali (1992: 117–18) as: '. . . . aggressive and macho both in rhetoric and action . . . . [and enabling the conjoining of the] traditionalism of the old or lower middle class . . . . with the quasi-ethnic nationalism of male youth'. This sometimes leads to their involvement in crime; it is certainly implicated in their participation in public disorder and affray.

The public disturbances in Bradford, 1995[10]

Between 9 and 11 June 1995, three days of public disturbances took place in the mainly Muslim area of Manningham. Termed 'riots' by the media, they consisted of three days of violent disorder during which over 300 Pakistani Muslim youths rampaged on the streets, attacking the police station, throwing missiles (including petrol bombs) at passing cars, erecting burning barriers across roads, smashing windows and looting shops, wrecking garages and burning cars, fire-bombing businesses, pubs, clubs and an hotel and issuing death threats at knife point. The property damaged belonged to non-Muslims.

The Bradford Commission described the immediate reasons for the disturbances as:

> . . . . a failure to police by consent, and a widespread local misunderstanding of the accepted protocol for protest. The police showed their ignorance of the local population, and of its concerns; the protesters showed their ignorance of the means of acceptable protest; some representatives of the local population showed their ignorance of necessary and proper police procedures (Allen and Barrett 1996: 11).

The actual flashpoint to the 'riots' involved Muslim youths playing football on the street, police intervening and local people becoming involved in the ensuing rowdiness. Accounts of the incident vary: local people say the police tried to break up what was no more than a noisy game of football; the police refer to 'provocative swearing' and resistance to arrest by 'known troublemakers'. One of the young men's sisters (and her baby) joined the ensuing mêlée and this became a key factor in the subsequent disturbances. Rumours spread rapidly that the police had attacked an Asian woman and her baby and assaulted an Asian man by driving a car over his foot (subsequent medical examination found no evidence to support the charges). These rumours became the basis for public protest and eventual violent disorder.

Some aspects of the 1995 public disturbances in Bradford merit comment. First, the West Yorkshire police mishandled the situation, showing no understanding of the Muslim community and failing to differentiate between genuinely concerned people and criminal gangs. A massive failure of communication – or indeed any attempt to communicate – runs through the entire event. Secondly, though men and women of all ages protested outside the police station, the subsequent disorders were conducted solely by young Pakistani Muslim men. The involvement of older men – elders, community leaders and councillors –

was restricted to unsuccessful attempts to negotiate between police and protesters, and women's involvement consisted of a peace-making attempt by a group of 'interfaith' women. Thirdly, the young men's experience of a 'successful' campaign against prostitution had provided them with valuable communication and organisation skills that they applied to rioting. This included the ability to mobilise young Muslim men from towns and cities in the surrounding area.[11]

Between 1995 and 2001

Contrary to the impression given in most of the national press, Bradford between 1995 and 2001 was not an oasis of multicultural peace. The *Daily Mail* reported Asian youth besieging Toller Lane police station (the site of the 1995 protests) on Bonfire Night in both 1997 and 1998. The article quotes Jan-Khan (later to become spokesman for the Manningham Residents' Association): 'A serious drugs and alcohol problem is growing, but the local Asian community is in denial' and 'local politicians have a vested interest in playing it down. There's a powder keg waiting to explode' (Goodwin 1998). In 1999, I noted that acts of aggression by young Pakistani men had become part of everyday life in Bradford; that these were targeted at both genders, all ages and all ethnic groups, but received little, if any, media publicity (Macey 1999a: 855). In 2001, a report written before the public disturbances referred to Muslim youth having developed a sense of immunity from the law and boasting that 'the police daren't touch them for fear they'll riot' (Ousley 2001: 11). The 2001 disturbances, then, may have come as a shock to the government and many people in the country; they came as no surprise to the residents of Bradford.

The public disturbances in Bradford, 2001

Although in this chapter I use material from the two Home Office reports that have been published on the public disturbances in Bradford, Burnley and Oldham (Cantle 2001; Denham 2001), I have chosen to concentrate mainly on 'local' material. I use mainly media reports and the comments of local people, some made directly to me, others taken from newspapers.

The chronological development of the 2001 disturbances is as follows. *April 14–15, Bradford, West Yorkshire*: a fight at a Hindu wedding led to rumours of attacks on the Asian community by the National Front (NF). The response was a series of arson attacks in the city. *May 26, Oldham, Greater Manchester*: 'rioting' took place after white attacks on Asian homes, again linked to the NF. *June 5, Leeds, West Yorkshire*: Asian 'rioting' took place after a local man accused the police of squirting him with CS gas.

June 23, Burnley, Lancashire: violent disorder involving fighting between Asian and white youths took place following a hammer attack on an Asian taxi driver. *June 29, Accrington, Lancashire*: four petrol bombings took place on white-owned businesses, a Catholic school and a car. Asian youths were seen running away from the crime scenes. *June 30, Accrington, Lancashire*: an arson attack took place on an Asian home whilst the family was in the house. *July 7–10, Bradford, West Yorkshire*: large-scale rioting by Asian youths took place following a rally against the NF. Thus, the violent public disturbances of 2001 started, and culminated, in Bradford in what has been described in the media as the worst urban rioting on the British mainland for 20 years. As noted above, none of this surprised the people of Bradford:

> . . . . there is an overarching belief around the city today that these riots were going to happen whatever efforts were made to head them off. There was clearly a determination in some quarters for Bradford not to be left out of the chain of racial violence which has wracked the North of England this summer. And it is clear that some wouldn't be happy unless the scale of it was 'bigger and better' than the incidents in Burnley and Oldham (*Bradford Telegraph and Argus* 2001).

The immediate backdrop to the July public disturbances in Bradford centred around the NF, members of which had been banned from marching in the city. Rumours that an NF rally was planned despite the ban brought Asian youths on to the streets to 'defend the community'. An assault on an Asian youth by white drunks was the immediate catalyst for the explosion of violent disturbances of an order predicted to cost the city between £7.5 and £10 million (Denham 2001) with policing costs of an additional £10 million.

The 2001 public disorders took a similar format to the 1995 ones: four to five hundred young Muslim men took to the streets armed with petrol bombs, stones, baseball bats and a variety of other weapons and missiles. Fires were lit in the middle of roads, and garages, businesses, pubs, clubs and cars owned by non-Muslims were set on fire. There were some differences between this year's disorders and the earlier ones: first, this time the rioters had prepared in advance, collecting baseball bats, knives and other weapons and storing petrol bombs in derelict houses around the city (Harris 2001). This goes some way towards explaining the second difference between the two disturbances, which is their extent, ferocity and the scale of injury and damage. Some 326 police were injured and there were a number of stabbings – including of police horses. Some 30 or more people were inside one of the clubs set on fire, yet the rioters deliberately tried to prevent their escape by blocking emergency exits with burning cars. A third difference is the increased involvement of young children in this disorder. One primary school teacher reported a six-year-old Muslim child, taking part in the routine Monday morning 'what I did this weekend' session, saying: '. . . . we made petrol bombs at my house, Miss'. A local reporter observed:

> A ten-year old boy, his face covered by a handkerchief, captured the reality of how deeply raw hatred has become embedded. Rage had so poisoned him he was prepared to hurl a brick the size of his head at rows of riot police poised to charge barely 30 feet away. There was no fear in this child's eyes, just anger hard to understand in one so young. Around him were at least 60 teenagers and men launching volleys of petrol bombs, sticks and rocks at the massed police ranks. Many of these outlaws were children, but they were not playing a child's game (Dutt 2001).

A fourth difference between the two sets of disorders is what appears to be retaliatory action by white youths. An Asian-owned restaurant in one of the outer suburbs was attacked and other minor incidents have been reported. Local white youths did not have a history of burning cars and businesses, but it now appears they may be copying young Muslim men's style of vandalism and violence. Many white Bradfordians talk of the dangers of a 'white backlash' and many Muslim Bradfordians reply: 'I don't blame them.'

Responses to, and 'explanations' of, the public disturbances

Most of the national press located the 'Bradford riots' in the context of disturbances in Accrington, Burnley, Leeds and Oldham and there was much talk of British National Party (BNP) and NF involvement. However, under the heading 'Now it's time for Bradford to stop making excuses', the local newspaper wrote:

> In our leading article after the Bradford Commission report into the Manningham riots [of 1995], we stated: 'In Bradford there is racial hatred; there is fear; there is ignorance; there is dire unemployment; there is poverty and deprivation; there is religious fundamentalism; there is political extremism; there is petty politics; there is ineptitude and incompetence; there is misplaced optimism; there is damaging pessimism and apathy; there are good intentions and there are evil ones'.

Five years on, can any reader put their hand on their heart and state in all honesty that anything has changed? . . . . at the root of everything there is still a fundamental and deep-seated hatred of white people and of authority in general in the hearts of a minority of young and mainly Muslim activists and thugs (*Bradford Telegraph and Argus* 2001).

The editorial goes on to say: 'criminal thuggery cannot be excused by deprivation or unemployment, by alleged police mistreatment or by provocation by the fascist scum of the National Front.' In this, the newspaper highlights some of the most frequently cited reasons, in academia and the media, for Pakistani Muslim young men's involvement in crime: material deprivation, unemployment, police mistreatment, racism, Islamophobia and the 'far right'. Before discussing these, it is interesting to note some local views on them:

Material deprivation and unemployment

Here everything in the Asian community is about keeping up with the Joneses. We have been here fifty years and we're going backwards. The Indian community is doing fine. It's the Pakistanis who are not making it (older Muslim man).

They talk about respect in our community, but if you've got money you've got respect. It's all about flash cars and pretty girls (young Muslim man).

It makes you sick when you see the Subarus and Porsches, all the flash cars they have up on Manningham (young white man).

Organised racism

Once again violence erupts on the streets of Bradford – and who is to blame? The police? The BNP? Society? Anyone but the so-called disaffected Asian youth, who feel they have the right to violate innocent people and use relentless thuggery to make themselves heard (older white man).

The NF are the only winners tonight. They've got exactly what they wanted. They will be sitting at home with a beer watching this on television and laughing (older Muslim man).

I have a sword ready at home and if some dumb bastard comes running towards me I will use it (young Muslim man).

Racism in the police

If it wasn't for the police there would have been some deaths. You can't blame the police – if they're too heavy-handed people complain, and if they don't do enough people say they're soft. They can't win (young Muslim man).

They should crack down on them hard, whether they're white or Asian. It's not a racial matter, it's plain law-breaking by idiots (older Muslim man).

It's not what they say and it's not what you think. It's about Asian lads shouting racism to keep the police off 'their' turf (young Muslim woman).

Racism and Islamophobia

The recent riots in Bradford were not to do with racial discrimination, poverty or whatever other excuse you may wish to pick out of thin air. The fact is that they were caused by young Asian thugs .... (older white man).

It's not about racism, it's about gangs, territory and control (young Muslim woman).

Our parents' generation were too tolerant. They took abuse and did nothing. Now we've got to sort out their mistakes (young Muslim man).

The above are only a small selection of local people's responses to the public disturbances in Bradford. There is no overall consensus of opinion, but there are interesting generational similarities *across* ethnic lines. This agreement is stronger in relation to 'answers' to the problem: 'send them back to Pakistan' is a comment made equally by whites and Asians, men and women! I will return to this later, but first evaluate some academic analyses of the 1995 public disorders in Bradford under the same headings.

Material deprivation and unemployment

The location of the public disturbances in Bradford – Manningham – is a materially deprived area and there is a clear correlation between deprivation – poverty, low-quality, overcrowded housing, low educational standards, unemployment – and young men's involvement in criminal activity. This is not least because these factors, especially unemployment, constitute a push to spend time on the streets, often in groups. Taj (1996: 5) remarks: 'Idle hands are the Devil's plaything and no serious commentator disputes the link between youth unemployment and anti-social behaviour.' Khan (1997: 18, 28) refers to a 'new Pakistani street culture' that he describes as 'highly macho' and linked to drug dependency and involvement in violent crime and prostitution. However, as I have noted elsewhere (Macey 1999a), material deprivation does not *in itself* constitute an explanation of public disorder and violence, since other residents of the area who share the same material environment have not resorted to such behaviour. Nor have white youths in comparable areas of deprivation – a fact commented on by Muslim men, including those currently in Armley goal for their involvement in the 2001 disturbances!

There are exceptionally high levels of unemployment in Manningham, some of which are undoubtedly due to racism (Allen and Barrett 1996; Ousley 2001). However, Taj (1996: 5) comments: '. . . . a proportion of the young people of the area make very unappealing prospective employees. They are the product of a cycle of low expectations and educational under-achievement. They offer few qualifications, lack skills and some display an offensive demeanour developed within their "street culture".' In Bradford, statistics for educational achievement by ethnicity mirror national ones (CBMC 2000; Farooq 2000), so that Pakistani Muslim boys achieve few public examination successes. To suggest that this is explicable by racism in schools is to beg the question of why Indian pupils and Pakistani Muslim girls do well in public examinations. However, the link between poor educational qualifications and unemployment, and between unemployment and crime, may help to explain young Muslim men's involvement in criminal activity in Bradford.

Organised racism

The BNP has racism at its core, but recently has developed a specifically anti-Islamic focus and targets areas with large Muslim populations. It gained a significant number of votes in the northern towns in which the 2001 disturbances took place. Husbands (1994) suggests that the real significance of the BNP, however, is not its electoral potential, but its role in creating a climate that facilitates racial antagonism and violence. Like the

NF, there is a clear association between its presence in an area and the growth of racially motivated violence, and this must be a factor in the clashes between white and Asian youths in Burnley and Oldham. The BNP has no base in Bradford and the NF had been banned from marching in the city on the day that public disorder broke out, yet the mere *threat* of the NF was the spark that lit what Jan-Khan called the 'powder keg'.

White extremist organisations with a racially divisive agenda are joined in Bradford by Muslim ones. In the aftermath of the 1995 disorders, one militant Muslim group – *Hizb-ut-Tahir* (HUT – Party of Liberation) – tried to rally support among Pakistani youth (Allen and Barrett 1996). The combination of political and religious zeolotry provided by such groups appeals to young men and, in the wake of the 2001 disturbances, HUT is again highly visible in Bradford. Husbands (1994) notes with reference to the BNP that the impact of such groups is not restricted to the numbers involved, but has wider effects on local populations, and Lewis (2001: 15) refers to HUT's circulation of 'inflammatory literature – anti-democratic, anti-zionist, anti-western, anti-Hindu, and anti-Sikh'. This is an example of the inadequacy of such explanations of violent public disorder as those that blame the BNP or NF. It illustrates the complexity of a reality in which both white *and* Muslim separatists contribute to the creation of mutually antagonistic ideologies that can predispose young men to violent confrontation.

Racism in the police

The police have been accused of carrying some responsibility for both the 1995 and the 2001 public disturbances in Bradford. Writing about the 1995 disorders, Burlet and Reid (1998) refer to many years of strained relations between the police and the Pakistani Muslim community; the Bradford Commission suggests that this created a disposition to violence; and Taj (1996: 8) comments: '. . . . it is impossible to overstate the mistrust with which younger members of the community viewed the police.' The two Home Office reports on the 2001 disturbances adopt a more positive approach, and Cantle (2001: 40) observes that '. . . . there has been a great deal of support for the police and a recognition that their approach has improved considerably, for example since the earlier riots in Bradford in 1995'. Denham (2001: 17) notes, however, '. . . . that there are policing issues which need to be addressed'.

There is a large literature on racism in the police in general, in relation to young men in particular and with reference to public disorder/riots (Benyon 1986; Jewson 1990; Cashmore and McLaughlin 1991; Macpherson 1999). However, as I have previously observed (Macey 1999a), there are aspects of the relationship between the police and Pakistani Muslim men in Bradford that should make one cautious of an uncritical acceptance of police racism as being responsible for young men's involvement in crime and public disorder. For example, such cultural traditions as arranged marriages are sometimes abused in ways that bring the police and Muslim men into conflict. *Forced* marriage is far more common in Bradford than is suggested by such publications as *A Choice by Right* (Home Office 2000b), and women who resist often turn to the police for help. This also applies to women fleeing domestic violence, which is more common than the Muslim community acknowledges (Keighley Domestic Violence Forum 1998; Macey 1999b). Refusal by the police to return unwilling women to their homes sometimes culminates in violence, as brothers, cousins and friends mobilise wider networks to search for 'offending' women. It is notable in this context that the West Yorkshire police force was one of the first in the country to take seriously the issue of domestic violence and to implement radical policies on it (Hanmer and Saunders 1993). Other examples of conflict between the police and Muslim men centre around the concept of *izzat* and the use of religion to justify threatened or actual violence against people seen as offending against Islam. I noted above the campaign against prostitutes, violence against gay men and lesbians, domestic violence and murder.

There are, then, a number of issues, many involving gender, that are a source of tension between the police and Muslim men. These mean that the interests of the latter would be served if the police become sufficiently nervous of accusations of racism as to be unwilling to intervene in 'community affairs'. This is illustrated by an alternative explanation of the 1995 disturbances put forward by young Muslim women, which is that the disturbances were used by rival gangs as part of the battle for control of territory, drugs and prostitution with the aim of making Manningham a 'no-go' area for the police. These young women also offered an alternative explanation to the usual 'racism' one of the disproportionate use of 'stops and searches' against black and Asian young men (Home Office 2000a). One woman laughed at my question about the police targeting young Asian men for searches, saying: 'Well, they would, wouldn't they? After all they know it's these lads who're doing the dealing.' Finally, in response to a question about racism in the police as a cause of the 1995 rioting, one woman stated that 'the lads' had planned to accuse the police of racism because this had worked in the past. Similar points are being made in relation to the 2001 disturbances. Writing in the local paper, Greenhalf (2001) comments: 'there are young Muslim men in Bradford for whom rioting is an expression of power, not anger.' He quotes Allan Brack, a former race relations worker and director of Bradford Festival, as saying:

The Muslim disturbances of 1995 were about territory; the Muslim rioting over the weekend was about male chauvinism and, it has to be admitted, Muslim racism.

These lads want to drive out non-Muslims; it's a form of ethnic cleansing. The white middle class, which has been in a state of denial about this trend, will be appalled that this has happened; but, after seven years of inaction by the authorities and softly-softly policing, this has been brewing up (ibid.).

In sum, the West Yorkshire police force undoubtedly contains both institutional racism and some racist officers. However, the factors noted above need to be considered before police racism is too readily accepted as a major cause of Pakistani Muslim young men's involvement in public disorder.

Racism and Islamophobia

As with racism in the police, there is clear evidence of racism, institutional racism, racial disadvantage and discrimination in British society and, by definition, in Bradford. These extend across all spheres: the criminal justice system, education, employment, health, housing and social services. Racism also includes verbal harassment, physical violence and murder (for an overview of racism in Britain, see Modood *et al* 1997; for discussion of the situation in Bradford, see Allen and Barratt 1996; Ratcliffe 1996; Ousley 2001). The extent and impact of racism should never be underestimated: whether overt or cover, it is a pernicious force that blights the lives of all British citizens – and results in the deaths of some of them. Because of this, racism is too important to be trivialised by the indiscriminate use of the concept to 'explain' every situation in which black or Asian people are disadvantaged relative to white ones. Disadvantage is not the same thing as discrimination and it is not always the result of racism. Sometimes, the cultural and/or religious practices of minority ethnic groups are implicated in their disadvantage.

Similar points apply to the currently fashionable term 'Islamophobia' (Conway 1997). There is no doubt that many people in Britain view Islam through the stereotypical lens of media representation as a monolithic religion that is cruel and barbaric, homophobic and misogynist – and profoundly anti-western.[12] Whether the extent or magnitude of this justifies the term 'phobia' is debatable, as is the utility of the concept in the struggle against racism. The stage has been reached where the accusation of 'Islamophobia' is levelled at anyone who appears to criticise Islam or Muslim behaviour. At the risk of being labelled Islamophobic, I discuss below some aspects of Islam, or its cultural interpretation, which may be implicated in the crimes committed by Muslims, specifically young Muslim men in Bradford.

Islam, culture and crime

It can be suggested that the link between Islam and crime is both direct and indirect: the former when Muslims commit (or justify) crime in the name of Islam, the latter when Islamic doctrine (or its cultural interpretation) operates to put Muslims in situations commonly seen as predisposing people to criminal activity. Examples of the former include physical violence against women, gay men, lesbians and prostitutes and speeches and writings that come close to incitement to racial hatred. Of these, only acts of physical violence against women are specifically stated in the *Qu'ran* to be acceptable within limitations (Mather 1998); the others involve cultural interpretations of *Qu'ranic* edicts that carry the *potential* to be translated into violent action. These include condemnation of homosexuality and definitions of approved gender relationships and appropriate sexual behaviour. They also include the proselytising (or missionary) requirement that is a logical outcome of defining Islam as the only true faith.

Islam is not, of course, the only religion that believes it has a monopoly over truth and salvation. It is, as far as I am aware, the only faith that divides the world into good and evil, *Dar al-Islam* (the Domain of Islam) and *Dar al-Harb* (the Domain of War, i.e. the non-Muslim world). Arguably, this impacts negatively on both inter-faith and inter-ethnic relations and is implicated in the adoption of anti-western attitudes and behaviour by some Muslims. For example, I listened to a visiting Imam to the University of Bradford Islamic Society telling his audience that westerners 'promote indecency and immorality' and are 'responsible for starting and continuing the AIDS epidemic' (Macey 1999a). *The Manifesto of the Muslim Parliament of Great Britain* refers to the difficulty for Muslims of leading a *muttaqi* (God-fearing, pious) life in a 'corrupt' environment and speaks of the need to 'arrest the "integration" and "assimilation" of Muslims themselves into the corrupt bogland of Western culture and supposed civilization' (cited in Newbigin *et al* 1998). Other Islamic publications make such comments as 'there is nothing in Western societies that remotely resembles good behaviour' (Islamic Party of Britain); 'The West's aggression towards Muslims is well-documented' (*Al-Sahwa*); and '[the USA and Britain] speak honeyed words publicly, and sow corruption and injustice stealthily. A Machiavellian practise that is at the very heart of modern Judaeo-Christian culture' (*Al-Hujjat*) (cited by the London Bible

College, 1999). More immediately relevant to this chapter, perhaps, is Lewis's (2002: 16) observation of '. . . . the failure of the generality of the *ulama* to relate to British Muslims and take their questions seriously'. This leaves young men open to the influence of extremist groups whose ideology is profoundly anti-western and hence antagonistic to integration of any kind. It also renders them beyond the control of community elders and Imams.'

At a different level, there is a sense in which Islam exerts an indirect influence on criminal activity via aspects of its teaching (or their cultural interpretation) that affect the structural location of Muslims in British society. As noted above, large numbers of Muslims live in materially deprived, ethnically segregated areas in overcrowded, inadequate housing; male children underachieve in school; and there are high levels of unemployment, ill-health and poverty. Such areas are associated with crime, illegal drugs and violence and were the sites of the 1995 and 2001 public disturbances in Bradford. Some of this is explicable in socio-economic terms and some is a consequence of racism. But it can be suggested that Islam itself contributes to the situation in a number of ways.

For example, poor, overcrowded housing is not only due to racism by building societies and housing authorities, but is also connected to the Islamic prohibition on mortgages as usury. This, together with the cultural tradition of extended family living, goes some way towards explaining Muslim disadvantage in housing. It also helps to explain residential segregation by ethnicity, since buying a house without access to a mortgage tends to limit purchasers to poorer-quality, older housing, often located in particular parts of cities. This is exacerbated by chain migration and the tendency to establish *biradari* groups in close proximity to each other where the systems, structures and cultures of, for instance, rural Mirpur, are played out against the backdrop of urban Bradford (Ballard 1994).

Educational underachievement is not explicable in terms of racism alone, but is affected by such cultural factors as the preference for boys that leads to extreme permissiveness in their upbringing and the religious requirement for mosque attendance and the learning of Arabic. Long hours in mosques mean that many Muslim boys are extremely tired in school. The learning of Arabic impacts negatively on young boys' development of English language competence mainly because their home language is commonly not English (Farooq 2000). The situation is exacerbated by the cultural practice of removing children from school to spend extended periods in Pakistan.

Poverty itself is partly a consequence of Islamic definitions of appropriate gender roles, particularly the expectation that women's primary focus should be husbands, homes and families. This sometimes leads to the denigration of education for girls and young women and even the permanent removal of Muslim girls from school – with obvious consequences for their entry to the labour market. Sometimes women are discouraged, or actually prohibited, from working outside the home and this, together with the Muslim preference for large families, contributes to familial poverty, particularly given high male unemployment due to low educational qualifications and lack of skills.

Another cultural tradition that has a major impact on all the above factors is that of intercontinental marriages between British and Pakistani partners. In Bradford as many as 50 per cent of all marriages in the Pakistani Muslim community fall into this category which results, as Ousley (2001: 11) observes, in a constant intake of residents to the community who have little, or no, access to English and frequently no education or skills to enable them to participate in British society. It also results in the tendency for a particular, highly traditional, variant of Islam from rural Pakistan to be constantly replicated in urban Bradford (Macey 1999b). Taken in conjunction with Islamic definitions of women's roles and geographical segregation, this has both short- and long-term con-sequences for individuals and families, particularly in relation to Mirpuri brides. Young women who come to this country with no language or educational skills are prevented from participating in wider society, understanding the English education system or subsequently being aware of, or able to control, their sons' criminal activities. It is notable in this context that arranged inter-continental marriages are strongly opposed by young Muslim women, but requested by their male counterparts on the grounds that 'Mirpuri wives are more obedient and easier to control than English ones' (Beckett and Macey 2001: 312).

In the white community, the correlation between socioeconomic status and crime is well established and this is undoubtedly applicable to the Pakistani Muslim community in Bradford, which is predominantly working class (Samad 1991). In other words, Pakistani Muslim young men's involvement in crime is partially explicable in class, rather than ethnic or religious, terms. However, this raises the question of *why* Pakistani Muslims are not achieving social mobility and extricating themselves from poverty after half a century in Britain. And on this question, I am forced to conclude that whilst one of the answers is undoubtedly racism, this is not the whole explanation; that there are elements of religious and cultural tradition which militate against the progress of the Muslim community. These same elements are implicated in Muslim male crime, both directly and indirectly, and it is difficult to see how change can be brought about unless the community itself is willing to adapt in ways it currently shows no signs of doing. Policy-makers, at both the national and local state levels, need to acknowledge that incidents of 'rioting' and public affray are not simply a response to deprivation, marginalisation and white racism, but are the result of complex inter-sections and interaction between a large number of variables, some of them specifically related to cultural interpretations of Islam.

Conclusion

In this chapter I have analysed Pakistani Muslim young men's involve-ment in crime, particularly violent public disorder, in Bradford. Although these young men constitute only a tiny minority of the Pakistani Muslim population in Bradford, their criminal and neo-criminal behaviour is having a massive negative impact on the city and, indeed, on wider society. In Bradford, they are significantly adding to the city's already high level of poverty in a number of ways – both social and material – that have harmful short- and long-term consequences. These include exacerbating already high levels of ethnic division and tension; preventing young Muslim women from fulfilling their potential; 'driving out' young people from all ethnic groups (including white); increasing expenditure through policing bills and property repairs; and creating a negative image of the city that not only discourages inward investment and job creation, but is also causing established businesses to relocate. In terms of wider society, there is little doubt that the public disorders of 1995 and 2001 have exacerbated negative images of Islam in ways that could have long-term consequences for inter-ethnic and inter-faith relations.

For all these reasons, it is imperative that social science analyses of young Pakistani Muslim men's involvement in crime, including violent public disorder, are as comprehensive as possible. It is important, therefore, to consider the influences of gender, generation and social class, along with those of ethnicity and religion. We have to move on from explanations that focus only, or mainly, on racism and discrimination, whilst not negating their effects. We have to realise that ignoring cultural and religious influences on young Muslim men is perilously close to racism, first, in denying the strength and power of Pakistani culture and Islamic beliefs and, secondly, in assuming that these young men define themselves and situations only in relation to white institutions and structures. Overall, this can only produce inadequate accounts that are of little utility to changing the situation.

And change the situation we must, for everyone's sake, but particularly that of the children. For criminal young men are role models for young boys who are increasingly involved in anti-social and criminal behaviour: 'We made petrol bombs at my house, Miss' and 'My son looks at me, earning an honest living running this shop, and he looks at my car, which is not a good car – it's an old car. Then he looks at the young men on the street with their BMWs [from selling drugs]' (Muslim parent). But the question of *how* the situation can be changed for everyone's benefit is one to which there are no simple answers. I suggest, however, that Mitchell and Russell's (1994: 153–4) comment should form the bedrock of any proposals:

> . . . . the right to be different can never be unconditional . . . . No society can maintain a position in which 'anything goes' at the cultural level within its various communities. On the one hand, substantial sections of the population still appear to be unwilling to accept as citizens minorities that are culturally distinct and visibly different from themselves. On the other hand, some elements within the black and minority ethnic communities apparently wish to live apart, rejecting the view that the internalisation of some shared values and common commitments is the duty of every citizen.

This, together with research on Bradford and the observations of local people noted above, contains salutary lessons for individuals, communities and decision-makers at both local and national levels. Many, if not most, of these lessons carry radical imperatives to change and they are directed particularly at central government, the local authority, Muslim community leaders, mosques and Muslim parents. However, before change can take place the *need* for it has to be acknowledged and there are few signs this is the case in relation to young Pakistani Muslim men's involvement in crime in Bradford.

Notes

1 This position is apparently shared by the Foreign Office who recently threatened to remove funding from a research project unless a white researcher was replaced by one of Bangladeshi origin. Social scientists studying racialised relations in both Britain and the USA have long struggled with ethical and ideological issues to a degree that, I would suggest, has impacted adversely on the quality of research produced.

As a black American sociologist commented: 'It is apparent that much of our thinking about race and ethnicity is convoluted and otherwise blurred by ideological intrusions encouraging the use of folklore (Stanfield 1993: 33–4). For example, there have been major battles around the question of who has the right to research whom and this has led, at times, to the notion that one should only research, and write about, one's own ethnic group, or gender, or . . . . Another convention in this field is the pressure to focus only on white racism and to avoid analysing minority cultures and their possible impact on disadvantage.

Problems have also been created by the adoption of the generic term 'black' that, for a long time, dominated theory and research. Even the term 'Asian' was frowned upon for its potential to detract from what was seen as a common black cause and was thus labelled racist. Currently, anyone who insists on the necessity of disaggregating the category 'Asian' in the interests of knowledge and accuracy is accused of Islamophobia. These issues are discussed in some depth elsewhere (Allen and Macey, 1995; Macey 1999a, 1999b).

2   Whilst my account will also be partial, its aim is to highlight a number of issues that are commonly ignored. To this end, wherever possible I use empirical research focused particularly on Asian women in Bradford (Macey 1999a, 1999b), material from local sources and data from Asian academics.

3   Individuals, groups and institutions are all affected by Muslim youth crime: white young people are harassed on foot or in cars and suffer increasing levels of physical assaults; stones thrown through bus windows have resulted in services being withdrawn. African-Caribbean youth clubs are regularly vandalised, their members are taunted with shouts of 'slaves' and they are subjected to serious physical assault that has included murder. They view these actions as designed to drive them out of the city – a view confirmed by the perpetrators. Hindu and Sikh elderly day centres have been attacked and vandalised and these groups, too, view Muslim violence as aimed at driving them out of Bradford. The university's student recruitment has been adversely affected by media coverage of 'rioting' and recent events resulted in the withdrawal of a group of Indian (Hindu) students due to concern for their personal safety. More generally, white students report increasing levels of harassment and physical assault. All this has a negative impact on a city that is already among the most deprived in Britain. The university, for example, is one of the biggest employers in the city, in addition to which a great deal of local business is dependent on it.

Another aspect of the current situation that has potentially serious long-term consequences is the city's loss of its most talented young people. White and Indian youths have spoken to me of their plans to leave Bradford as soon as possible and several white youngsters have said that they do not admit to 'outsiders' that they live in Bradford. A recent survey of sixth-form students in the city found that only one-third of them thought that the city would have improved in five years' time; one-third also thought that racialised relations would have further deteriorated (Wainwright 2001).

4   *Biradaris* are patrilineal kinship groupings. In Mirpur these are linked to status in a way that owes more to Hindu than Muslim ideology. In Britain, social

exchanges, organised by and through female members of the family, are crucial to the maintenance and extension of *biradaris* (Shaw 1994).

5   This section rests heavily on the Bradford Commission report (Allen and Barrett 1996). See also Ratcliffe (1996) and Samad (1992).

6   1) 'White' is, not, of course, an ethnic group, despite its use as such in most official statistics; 2) the white population in Bradford includes sizeable populations of people of, for example, Polish and Lithuanian origin; and 3) the population of Bradford also includes people defined as Black African, Black Other, Chinese, Other-Asian and Other-Other. I have not included these groups in the table because I do not refer to them in this chapter.

7   These statistics are likely to underestimate the Pakistani population, both currently and in terms of predicted numbers. One of the reasons for this is the government's waiving in 1997 of the 'primary purpose rule'. This has resulted in a significant increase in the number of intercontinental marriages and around 700 marriages a year involve partners from Bradford and Pakistan (CBMC 1996b).

8   Less publicly, local politics have long been manipulated as male family members tell non-English-speaking women how to vote. This has been exacerbated by the extension of postal voting and one of my Pakistani women students innocently related how she was prevented from voting 'Green' at the general election by her uncle's collection of all the family's voting cards to support the Conservatives.

9   To categorise such examples of harassment as a 'minor nuisance' is, of course, to ignore the distress caused to victims, as well as the impact on their behaviour. I know of cases where telephone abuse has resulted in parents subsequently restricting daughters' freedom. In the case of harassment in public places, a large number of women students change their routes to avoid known gathering places of young Muslim men.

10 This section rests heavily on the Bradford Commission report (Allen and Barrett 1996).

11 More detailed accounts of the 1995 public disorders can be found in Taj (1996) and Foundation 2000 (1995).

12 Such stereotypes have, of course, been reinforced by the recent terrorist attack on the USA. The situation is not helped by those Muslims who have stated on television that they are not British Muslims, but Muslims in Britain and that their loyalty is, therefore, to Muslims in other parts of the world.

References

Afshar, H. (1989) Gender roles and the 'Moral economy of kin' among Pakistani women in West Yorkshire. *New Community* 15(2): 211–25.

Afshar, H. (1994) Muslim women in West Yorkshire: growing up with real and imaginary values amidst conflicting views of self and society. In H. Afshar and M. Maynard (eds.) *The Dynamics of 'Race' and Gender: Some Feminist Interventions.* London: Taylor & Francis, pp. 127–47.

Ali, Y. (1992) Muslim women and the politics of ethnicity and culture in northern England. In G. Sahgal and N. Yuval-Davis (eds.) *Refusing Holy Orders: Women and Fundamentalism in Britain*. London: Virago, pp. 101–23.

Alibhai-Brown (1998) God's own vigilantes. *The Independent* 12 October.

Allen, S. and Barrett, J. (1996) *The Bradford Commission Report* (the Bradford Congress). London: HMSO.

Allen, S. and Macey, M. (1995) Some issues of race and ethnicity in the 'new Europe': rethinking sociological paradigms. In P. Brown and R. Crompton (eds.) *The New Europe: Economic Restructuring and Social Exclusion*. London: UCL Press, pp. 108–35.

Al Sadaawi, N. (1991) Women in Islam. Paper presented to the *Women in Society Seminar Series*, University of Bradford.

Anwar, M. (1979) *The Myth of Return: Pakistanis in Britain*. London: Heinemann Educational Books.

Ballard, R. (1994) *Desh Pardesh: The South Asian Presence in Britain*. London: C. Hurst & Co.

Ballard, R. and Kalra, V. (1994) *The Ethnic Dimensions of the 1991 Census*. Manchester: Manchester University Census Group.

Barclay, G. and B. Mhlanga, B. (2000) *Ethnic Differences in Decisions on Young Defendants Dealt with by the Crown Prosecution Service*. London: Home Office, Section 95, Findings no. 1 (a Home Office publication under s. 95 of the Criminal Justice Act 1991).

Beckett, C. and Macey, M. (2001) Race, gender and sexuality: the oppression of multiculturalism. *Womens Studies International Forum* 24 (3): 309–19.

Benyon, J. (1986) *A Tale of Failure: Race and Policing*. Warwick: University of Warwick: Centre for Research in Ethnic Relations.

Bradford Telegraph & Argus (2001) Now it's time for Bradford to stop making excuses. Editorial 9 July.

Burlet, S. and Reid, H. (1998) A gendered uprising: political representation and minority ethnic communities. *Ethnic and Racial Studies* 21(2): 270–87.

Cantle, T. (2001) *Community Cohesion: A Report of the Independent Review Team*. London: HMSO (http://www.homeoffice.gov.uk/new.htm).

Cashmore, E. and McLaughlin, E. (eds.) (1991) *Out of Order? Policing Black People*. London: Routledge.

City of Bradford Metropolitan District Council (1993) *Areas of Stress within Bradford District*. Bradford: Research Section.

City of Bradford Metropolitan District Council (1996a) *Bradford & District Economic Profile 1996*. Bradford: Economic Information Service.

City of Bradford Metropolitan District Council (1996b) *Bradford & District Demographic Profile*. Bradford: Educational Policy & Information Unit.

City of Bradford Metropolitan District Council (1998) *Bradford & District Economic Profile July Update*. Bradford: Economic Information Service.

City of Bradford Metropolitan District Council (2000) *1997–1999 GCSE and Advanced Level Gender and Ethnic Group Analysis*. Bradford: Information and Planning.

Conway, G. (1997) *Islamophobia: A Challenge for us All.* London: The Runnymede Trust.

Denham, J. (2001) *Building Cohesive Communities: A Report of the Ministerial Group on Public Disorder and Community Cohesion.* London: HMSO. (http://www.homeoffice.gov.uk/new.htm).

Dutt, K. (2001) Where do we go from here? Riots special. *Bradford Telegraph & Argus* 9 July.

Farooq, Z. (2000) Ethnicity and educational achievement: Pakistani Muslim children in Bradford. BA dissertation, University of Bradford.

Foundation 2000 (1995) *Disturbances in Manningham: A Community Response – the Voices must be Heard.* Bradford: Foundation 2000.

Goodwin, J.A. (1998) The powder keg. *Daily Mail* 23 November.

Greenhalf, J. (2001) Facing up to the future. *Bradford Telegraph & Argus* 9 July.

Hanmer, J. and Saunders, S. (1993) *Women, Violence and Crime Prevention: A Community Study in West Yorkshire.* London: Gower.

Harris, P. (2001) Far right picks next race target. *The Observer* 1 July.

Harris, R. (1998) Bangladeshis in London. Paper presented at the Institute for Public Policy Research's 'Community flashpoints and young British Muslims' *Seminar on Young British Muslims*, London.

Hickman, M. and Walter, B. (1997) *Discrimination and the Irish Community in Britain.* London: Commission for Racial Equality.

Home Office (2000a) *Statistics on Race and the Criminal Justice System.* London: HMSO.

Home Office (2000b) *A Choice by Right: The Report of the Working Group on Forced Marriage.* London: HMSO.

Hood, R. (1992) *Race and Sentencing in the Crown Court.* London: Clarendon Press.

Husbands, C. (1994) Following the 'continental model'? Implications of the recent electoral performance of the British National Party (BNP). *New Community* 20(4): 563–79.

Institute for Public Policy Research (1998) 'Community flashpoints and young British Muslims' *Seminar on Young British Muslims*, London.

Jewson, N. (1990) Inner city riots. *Social Studies Review* 5(5): 170–74.

Kassam, N. (ed.) (1997) *Telling It Like It Is: Young Asian Women Talk.* London: Livewire Books/The Women's Press.

Keighley Domestic Violence Forum (1998) *Conference on Domestic Violence in Asian Communities.* Bradford: KDVF/University of Bradford.

Khan, A. (1997) An examination of drug use within the 'Pakistani' community in Bradford. BA Dissertation, University of Bradford.

Khanum, S. (1992) Education and the Muslim girl. In G. Sahgal and N. Yuval-Davis (eds.) *Refusing Holy Orders: Women and Fundamentalism in Britain* London: Virago, pp. 124–40.

Lewis, P. (1994) *Islamic Britain.* London: I.B. Tauris.

Lewis, P. (2001) British Muslims and the search for religious guidance. In J. Hinnells and W. Menski (eds.) *From Generation to Generation: Religious Reconstruction in the South Asian Diaspora.* Forthcoming.

London Bible College (1999) *The Westophobia Report: Anti-Western and Anti-Christian Stereotyping in British Muslim Publications. Occasional Paper* 1, September. London: LBC Centre for Islamic Studies and Muslim-Christian Relations.

Macey, M. (1999a) Class, gender and religious influences on changing patterns of Pakistani Muslim male violence in Bradford. *Ethnic and Racial Studies* 22(5): 845–66.

Macey, M. (1999b) Religion, male violence and the control of women: Pakistani Muslim men in Bradford. *Gender and Development* 7(1): 48–56.

Macpherson, Sir William of Cluny (1999) *The Stephen Lawrence Inquiry.* London: Home Office (Cm. 42621).

Mather, Y. (1998) Gender and Islamic fundamentalism. Paper presented at the *Gendering the Millennium International Conference*, University of Dundee.

Miller, J., Bland N. and Quinton P. (2000) *The Impact of Stops and Searches on Crime and the Community.* Police Research Paper 127. London: HMSO.

Mitchell, M. and Russell, D. (1994) Race, citizenship and 'Fortress Europe' In P. Brown and R. Crompton (eds.) *A New Europe? Economic Restructuring and Social Exclusion.* London: UCL Press.

Modood, T., Berthoud, R., Lakey, J., Nazroo, J., Smith, P., Virdee, S. and Beishon, S. (1997) *Ethnic Minorities in Britain: Diversity and Disadvantage.* London: Policy Studies Institute.

Newbigin, L., Sanneh, L. and Taylor J. (1998) *Faith and Power: Christianity and Islam in a 'Secular' Britain.* London: SPCK.

Ousley, Sir Herman (2001) *Community Pride not Prejudice: Making Diversity Work in Bradford.* Bradford: Bradford Vision.

Patel, P. (1998) Southall black sisters. Keynote address to the conference on *Domestic Violence in Asian Communities*, University of Bradford/Keighley Domestic Violence Forum.

Phillips, C. and Brown, D. (1998) *Entry into the Criminal Justice System: A Survey of Police Arrests and their Outcomes.* Home Office Research Study 185. London: HMSO.

Ratcliffe, P. (1996) *'Race' and Housing in Bradford.* Bradford: Bradford Housing Forum.

Samad, Y. (1991) Book burning and race relations: political mobilisation of Bradford's Muslims. *New Community* 18(4): 507–19.

Samad, Y. (1998) Muslims, media and multiculturalism in Bradford. Paper presented at the *Seminar on Young British Muslims*, Institute for Public Policy Research, London.

Shaw, A. (1994) The Pakistani community in Oxford. In R. Ballard (ed.) *Desh Pardesh: The South Asian Presence in Britain.* London: C. Hurst & Co., pp. 35–57.

Singh, R. (1994) Introduction. In Bradford Heritage Recording Unit, *Here to Stay: Bradford's South Asian Communities.* Bradford: BHRU.

Stanfield, J.H. II (1993) Epistemological considerations. In J.H. Stanfield II and R.M. Dennis (eds.) *Race and Ethnicity in Research Methods.* London: Sage, pp. 16–36.

Taj, M. (1996) *A 'Can Do' City: Supplementary Observations, Comments and Recommendations to the Bradford Commission Report.* Bradford: Taj.

Virdee, S. (1995) *Racial Violence and Harassment.* London: Policy Studies Institute.

Wainwright, M. (2001) Youth survey offers hope to battered city. *Guardian* 11 July.

West Yorkshire Police (2001) *Chief Constable's Annual Report 1999–2000.* Wakefield: West Yorkshire Police Authority.

Women Against Fundamentalism (1998) *Free Zoora Shah!* London: WAF.

Chapter 3

Muslim women's safety talk and their experiences of victimisation: a study exploring specificity and difference

Basia Spalek

Introduction

Within the discipline of criminology, a large amount of research has been conducted into both the fear of crime and victimisation. Nonetheless, much of the work here has failed to capture the particularities of individual experience. Surveys have often been carried out in which individuals have been grouped according to very general categories such as gender, class or race and yet there may be important differences between the persons who have been grouped together within a general category. This is particularly significant when looking at the issue of race, since the categories used to define individuals are in many cases so general that they obscure significant religious and cultural differences. So, for example, the category 'Asian' glosses over the differences in experiences between individuals practising different faiths. Indeed, the issue of religion has rarely, if ever, been raised by criminologists, due in part to the privileging of scientific and so-called objective discourses over less rational, less easily quantifiable knowledge claims.

This chapter presents the results of a study that explored the fear of crime and experiences of crime of a group of Muslim women of Pakistani, Bangladeshi and Indian origin living in Birmingham who wear the Hijab. It is argued here that greater specificity is needed in criminological work in order more fully to document individual experience. The results reported in this chapter illustrate that, for the women who took part in this research study, the Muslim religion they practise is intimately bound to their experiences of crime and their management of anxiety around crime. The main themes raised here include an analysis of veiling and its relationship with the women's safety talk, the impact of veiling upon men's behaviour in public space in terms of harassment and intimidation, and women's experiences of religious and racial harassment and abuse.

Fear of crime research

As a result of its modern roots, criminological discourse has traditionally imposed specific parameters on how we are to understand crime and victimisation. The issue of religion has often been ignored because people's beliefs do not easily fit into a framework that seeks to be so-called 'objective' and 'rational'. Taking a look first at the issue of fear of crime, this is a particular discourse that emerged in criminology during the 1960s in America and 1980s in England. Since that time, over two hundred articles, conference papers, monographs and books (Hale 1992: 1) have been written on this topic, illustrating how fear of crime has become a problem in its own right, over and above the study of crime. Research into fear of crime first appeared in public opinion polls in America, which asked citizens to pick out the social problems they paid most attention to. For example, a Gallop poll in 1963 revealed that out of a list of 39 problems, juvenile delinquency was the second most popular choice (President's Commission on Law Enforcement and Administration of Justice 1967: 50). Fear entered the criminological domain in 1967, when the President's Commission on Law Enforcement carried out a crime survey asking people about a range of crime issues, including fear of crime. According to this commission, fear of crime was a fear of stranger attack: 'The fear of crimes of violence is not a simple fear of injury or death or even of all crimes of violence, but at bottom, a fear of strangers' (ibid.: 50).

The commission's survey first appeared at a time of civil unrest amongst black citizens in America, when mass riots occurred. The Watts riot in Los Angeles in 1965 killed 34 people, injured 1,032 and property was destroyed to the sum of approximately $40 million (ibid.: 32). The stranger who was feared was the black rioter protesting against racial injustice, who attacked 'policemen, white passers-by, and white-owned commercial establishments' (ibid.). Fear of stranger attack came to be adopted by many other criminologists, so that this became the main paradigm through which fear of crime was viewed. The question most commonly used in surveys to try to quantify fear levels is: 'Is there anywhere around here – that is within a mile – where you would be afraid to walk at night?' (Eve 1985: 404).[1]

Feminist work has made a significant contribution to fear of crime research. Feminist studies illustrate that, when examining women's fear of crime, it is important to transcend the public/private distinction (Walklate 2001). In particular, radical feminist research reveals that underpinning women's anxiety about crime is a fear of men, since women often have to live around daily harassments and threats to personal security from male intimates, acquaintances and strangers (Stanko 1985). The root of fear of crime is the fear of sexual danger. Women routinely learn to negotiate their lives around harassment, incest, violence and rape. These experiences cannot be separated according to a public and private distinction. Feminist analyses have therefore broadened the lens through which fear of crime has been viewed within criminology in order to include private as well as public violence and intimidation.

Clearly, then, an important aspect of feminist work has been to highlight the extent of male violence against women and to show that underpinning women's fear of crime is a fear of sexual violence and harassment. However, it might be argued that feminist analyses have insufficiently taken into account the notion of difference. Although black feminists have argued for increased awareness of religious and cultural differences (Mama 1990), the predominant focus of western feminism has been upon white women (Maynard 1994). Even where research has included women of colour, this has largely been done to highlight the shared experiences of women in general – that of male violence and its potential. Although implicit in feminist accounts may be an acknowledgement of there being differences between women, there is little discussion of what difference means and of how this may be incorporated into empirical research (ibid.). It seems that studies with female researchers and women as the researched group have largely omitted differences amongst women (Bhavani 1994). Walklate (2001) argues that a postmodern feminist position on women's fear of crime avoids making any claims or statements on women in general. Rather, the specificity and diversity of experiences is recorded, whilst acknowledging that there may be certain similarities between different groups of women. For example, it might be argued that the fear of rape or sexual assault underpins most women's anxiety towards crime (ibid.).

Differences may stem from race, ethnicity, class, age, sexuality and so forth (Maynard 1994). Targeting one particular aspect of difference is problematic since the many dimensions to difference overlap. For example, discrimination based on race may intersect with discrimination based on religion, sexuality and so on (Franks 2000). Indeed, a recent study on religious discrimination by Weller *et al* (2001: 12) found that interviewees who were members of minority ethnic groups often felt that in practice religious and racial discrimination were not separable. None the less, individuals whose appearance was an expression of their faith (as in the case of Muslim women and Sikh men) were able to establish clear differences between racial and religious discrimination. Taking a look at the present research study, the race, age, gender, class, etc., of the women who were interviewed, as well as the religion they practise, are all important factors underpinning the women's experiences. The research study reported here essentially focused upon three main 'structures' impacting upon the women's experiences: race, religion and gender. It is important to stress that most of the women who were interviewed were of Pakistani or Bangladeshi origin. This is because the main Muslim group in Britain consists of people from Pakistan and Bangladesh (Joly 1995). This means that instances of racial, as well as religious, harassment and abuse were documented by the researcher. Ten Muslim women living in the Birmingham area who wear the Hijab were interviewed at length and questions were asked about their personal safety, their views on crime, and any experiences of victimisation. The women were aged between 19 and 30. The interviews took place between May 2001 and December 2001. Importantly, on 11 September a series of terrorist attacks were committed in the USA, which were linked to an Islamic terrorist organisation, al-Qaida. These attacks had serious repercussions upon Muslim communities in the western world in that many individuals were attacked (some were killed) or subjected to abuse, and mosques also became the targets of hate crime. The interview data as presented here, therefore, include experiences of harassment and violence in the aftermath of the attacks in America. The data reveal that the Muslim faith not only informed individuals' perceptions of crime, risk from crime and victimisation, but it was also a fundamental aspect of this group of women's experiences of crime and victimisation.

Research methods

A qualitative research approach was taken through the use of in-depth interviews. In-depth interviews allow a subject to express him or herself more fully, with answers not being as dependent upon categories constructed as part of the creation of a questionnaire (Maykut and Morehouse 1994). There are several aspects to the research study reported in this chapter that might be defined as feminist. First, the focus of the research was that of women and, as the study was examining fear of crime and victimisation, how women's lives are constrained by the actions of men (Kelly *et al* 1994). At the same time, however, an important aspect of the research study reported here was that of a focus upon women's agency. In other words, how did the women who were interviewed manage their lives around violence (or the threat of violence) from men? This focus upon how women resist and challenge masculinity and male dominance has been highlighted by other researchers as an important element of feminist research (Bhavani 1994; Kelly *et al* 1994). The issue of difference was also tackled in this research study as a response to the criticism targeted at feminist research that it has failed to address difference sufficiently, focusing research almost exclusively on white women. The study reported here tried to document the victimisation experiences and the fear of crime of a group of Muslim women of Pakistani and Bangladeshi origin in order to introduce greater diversity and specificity into these two important areas within criminology. Through looking at the specific experiences of a group of Muslim women, as opposed to the experiences of Asian women in general, it was found that particular aspects of their victimisation and fear of crime were explored which would otherwise not have been.

Feminist researchers call for the researcher to acknowledge that he or she may be in a position of power over the researched as participants may be asked to reveal sensitive/intimate information (Renzetti and Lee 1993). The researcher herself was a 'white', 'non-Muslim' woman. 'Being white' was problematic since it might be argued that this placed the researcher in a position of power and privilege over the interviewees as a result of being in a social system which normalises racial inequality (Brown 1999). Being white is 'constituted in opposition to its subordinated other, the not-white, the not-privileged' (Lewis and Ramazanoglu 1999: 23). As a result, the researcher considered it to be important not to reproduce dominant (mis)representations of Muslim women and to present the stories of the women who took part in the study as accurately as possible. The in-depth interviews that were conducted took the format of a two-way conversation in which the interviewer would reveal information about herself. This was done in order to try to reduce the power differential through self-disclosure, which involves being open to any questions the interviewee may ask (Renzetti and Lee, 1993). As will be highlighted later on in this chapter, dominant media and social representations of Muslim women who wear the Hijab have tended to consist of the view that Muslim women are repressed and controlled by Muslim men. The findings of this research study illustrate that Muslim women who veil may actively choose to do so, and that veiling may be a liberating experience for them as this can free them from the male (sexual) gaze.

The researcher also cast a critical gaze over the issue of 'being white' in terms of any differences between her own experiences and those of the interviewees. It might be argued that 'whiteness' can provide protection from racial harassment and discrimination, since whiteness brings the privilege of inclusion (Lewis and Ramazanoglu 1999). As one young Sikh man is reported to have said, 'You can't appreciate racism unless you've experienced it' (Weller *et al* 2001: 20). Since the researcher had not directly experienced racial discrimination, it may be the case that some of the interviewees did not disclose the full extent of their discrimination, particularly when the researcher held a privileged racial identity. Similarly, the full extent of harassment and abuse as a result of being Muslim may not have been disclosed to the non-Muslim researcher. None the less, the researcher felt an intimate connection with the interviewees with respect to the issue of men. It seems that actual and potential violence and harassment from men frames most women's lives and so these experiences can transgress race and religious identities.[2] At the same time, however, it is important to acknowledge the racial and religious differences between the researcher and the researched, and to be aware that the writing in this chapter is framed by western academic standards and conventions. Fitting Muslim experiences into western frameworks of understanding is in itself problematic (Said 1981), and the research presented here can be criticised on this basis. A further point to make is the difficulty experienced by the non-Muslim researcher in understanding theological interpretations of aspects of Islam. The researcher relied heavily on the Muslim women's own interpretations of Islam, but also incorporated religious and cultural textbooks/research papers on Muslim experiences in order to help frame the research findings. Frequently, Muslim women and organisations were consulted regarding the nature of the various arguments developed in this study.

Islam, veiling and self-identity

A plethora of studies have examined the role that veiling plays in the lives of Muslim women (Watson 1994; Mohammad 1999; Franks 2000; Ghazal Read and Bartowski, 2000). These studies highlight the complexity of meanings conveyed by the Hijab, which suggests that different women have different interpretations regarding what veiling means to them. For the women taking part in the research study reported in this chapter, there are many dimensions to the issue of veiling. One aspect of veiling is that the Hijab itself is symbolic of Islam, and therefore represents an important facet of the woman's self-identity. As an example of this, the following quotation from an interview can be used here: 'It's like we shouldn't have to say we are Muslim, people should know automatically that you are

Muslim. That's also why they say you should wear a scarf and veil so that people can differentiate you from other religions and other identities.'

The interviewees also spoke about a 'hierarchy of identities' in which the Muslim identity occupies the dominant position, followed by the cultural background of the woman. This is because Islam is seen as uniting different cultures. Thus, one woman argued that 'There is a hierarchy of identity with Muslim being at the top, but you present that in the way you look'. Another woman clearly stated that she would not classify herself as being British Asian, such was her connection to Islam:

> I think that I would just classify myself as a Muslim because in Islam we are not supposed to have a nationality. We're not supposed to be nationalist. That is haram for us, we're not allowed to do that. United through Islam, doesn't matter what colour you are, what country you come from. So I wouldn't classify myself as British Asian.

The above interview extracts suggest that for these women the category 'Asian' is far too general and does not include the identity they connect most strongly to. Lazreg (1988) argues that difference has, in general, been extremely problematic for western social science from its very inception. General categories have often been created which have obscured specific identities and therefore experiences. In both national and local crime surveys, religion has rarely featured as a way of grouping individuals together; rather, ethnic identity has been the predominant method of classification. For example, the British Crime Survey, which documents the extent of victimisation and (amongst other things) the level of fear of crime amongst individuals, classifies people as belonging to Indian, Pakistani or Bangladeshi ethnic identities. In this way, the issue of religion is largely bypassed. As a result, the issue of religious discrimination and harassment is not directly raised (only indirectly within a general discussion about racial harassment) and the findings of the British Crime Survey are relayed predominantly in terms of a general 'Asian experience'. For example, in terms of anxiety related to crime, 41 per cent of Asian and 37 per cent of Black respondents were found to be very worried about their home being burgled, compared to 18 per cent of white respondents, in the British Crime Survey 2000 (Kershaw et al 2001: 48). Similarly it has been found that, in general, Asians are more likely to feel unsafe both out alone and in their homes after dark (Fitzgerald and Hale 1996: 3). Through using such a general category as 'Asian', the research may be reproducing the assumption that 'white' experiences constitute the norm whereas the individuals who lie outside the 'white' category constitute the 'Other'. As Brah (1996: 24, in Mohammad 1999: 221–2) has noted, in Britain Asians have been regarded as being 'outsiders', as 'undesirable' who practise 'strange religions'. The use of the general category 'Asian' in research may therefore serve to reproduce prejudices and dominant assumptions. At the same time, this classification groups together people who may have very little in common in terms of religion; thereby it has the effect of obscuring specific experiences. The findings of the study reported here suggest that if the women had been defined purely as 'Asian', a core element of their lives would have been missed out from any analysis of their fear of crime or victimisation. As Islam is part of the everyday life of these women, it plays a significant role in the ways in which they negotiate their personal safety, as will now be discussed in greater detail.

Veiling, the negotiation of difference and the management of male heterosexuality

Muslim women in Britain have often been seen as oppressed women who are under the control of men (Franks 2000). Indeed, some Muslim clergy and Islamic elites currently prescribe veiling as a custom in which 'good' Muslim women should engage as they are held responsible for their families' honour (Ghazal Read and Bartowski 2000). In some communities women are directly policed by men. Pressure may be placed upon women for them to stay at home, searches may be organised to find young women who have run away from home and Islam may be cited as a justification for subjecting women to abuse and violence (Macey 1999).

Nonetheless, the women taking part in this study had all chosen to adopt the Hijab by themselves. They are therefore an example of an increasing number of young Muslim people in Britain who resort directly to the Qur'an and hadiths as a resource in Islam rather than accepting the traditional views passed down to them from their parents (Joly 1995). The interview data elicited two important, related, dimensions to the issue of veiling in relation to the negotiation of safety. First, the Hijab was regarded by the women as being liberating since it freed them from the male (sexual) gaze and indeed in some cases it led to a reduction in the level of harassment from men. This illustrates that the threat of male violence is part of the everyday lives of these women as it is a part of most, if not all, women (see Stanko 1997). At the same time, implicit within the women's accounts of veiling were ideas about how a Good Woman should behave so as to reduce risk of being the victim of male violence. Embedded within these women's safety talk were social judgements about how women should behave, since women are ultimately held responsible for men's behaviour. Links can be made here with the religious beliefs of the women who took part in this study, since many of the women viewed veiling as a way of managing male sexuality. It seems that the women's safety talk was intimately connected to the Islamic faith they follow.

Turning to the issue of veiling being a liberating experience, many of the women interviewed argued that the Hijab frees them from the male gaze, thereby making them feel more confident. For example 'I feel more confident walking around because the whole point of the scarf is that people don't look at your body, they look at your mind, that is the whole concept behind the Hijab, they don't have to look at you.'

Whilst a significant proportion of women argued that wearing the Hijab makes them stand out in public places because they look different, this was considered to be preferable to experiencing a male (sexual) gaze. Many of the interviewees agreed that, whilst the Hijab might make them look different, this was preferable to them being harassed and feeling intimidated by men:

> If you take that away from the equation, the woman's body, that's one less thing for men. If they do look at you they are not looking at you in the bad sense, they're looking at you because of what you are wearing as in a scarf or a veil or whatever.
> So does that make you feel safer in public spaces?
> Yes.

Underpinning the women's accounts of veiling was a particular viewpoint towards men. Men are ultimately to be feared because of the physical and sexual threat they pose. This finding further substantiates feminists' claims that a fear of violence and rape pervades the lives of most (if not all) women, regardless of age, class or race (Gardner 1995; Stanko 1997). One interviewee argued 'I think I'm dressing like this because I don't trust men but I also feel confident and comfortable in my clothes. . . . I think that most men, all men are like potential rapists. You can't trust any man, I wouldn't trust them.' Whilst another stated:

> Most women, I mean if I was walking down a dark alley and I saw a man I would instantly feel scared, I'd fear for my life. Most women feel like that and I feel like that. It's always in the back of your mind. Even in the daytime not necessarily in the dark so I do have that fear all of the time even though I have never had a bad experience. It's probably all the stories that you hear.

Another interviewee related wearing the Hijab to protecting herself from men:

It's religious in the sense that women are supposed to hide themselves, it's not right if a woman goes out into the streets wearing tight-fitting clothes. So it is religion-orientated, you should protect yourself by wearing these loose-fitting clothes . . . . It's like eh you know what men are like so you have to cover yourself.

A few of the women interviewed believed that by veiling they perhaps reduced their risk of being the victims of harassment or physical and sexual assault. One interviewee said: 'I think that if I said that clothes had a great impact on rape and stuff I would be incorrect but I do actually believe that the way you dress that has a main influence on whether you're attacked or not.' And another argued:

I think that I feel quite safe as in confidence wise, but you also feel insecurity as normal people would walking alone. It gives me a sense of that maybe they won't attack you because I am covered.
Because you are less exposed?
Yes.

The above quotations raise two important issues. One is the extent to which these women may have internalised community and societal values regarding what the Good Woman (Stanko 1997) should do to avoid physical and sexual violence. Bartky (1998: 30) argues that women's movements are more restrictive than men's:

Feminine faces, as well as bodies, are trained to the expression of deference. Under male scrutiny women will avert their eyes or cast them downward; the female gaze is trained to abandon its claim to the sovereign status of seer. The 'nice' girl learns to avoid the bold and unfettered staring of the 'loose' woman who looks at whatever and whomever she pleases.

It might be argued that under the dominant system of male heterosexuality, women stand before the male panoptical gaze (ibid.). Certain expectations are therefore placed on women in terms of how they look and how they behave, which in turn translate into women's own self-policing. Stanko (1997: 486) argues that in terms of avoiding harassment and violence from men, the Good Woman (which implies a law-abiding, middle-class woman) is expected not to 'walk down dimly lit alleyways . . . . carry her handbag close, hitchhike'. Women who do not conform to these behaviours may be judged as undeserving of societal protection and therefore undeserving victims (ibid.). Thus, the Good Woman will dress sensibly and be risk averse. Linked to this theme is the notion that embedded within women's safety talk is blame from both the self and the wider community if a woman should fall victim and be found to be behaving in a particular way not consistent with that of the Good Woman (ibid.).

The idea often expressed by the women who took part in the current research study, that wearing the Hijab may reduce their risk of victimisation, may reflect expectations from their local communities about how women should dress and behave in order to avoid harassment and violence from men. Many Muslims believe that the Qur'an is the actual Word of God that was recorded by Muhammad during the early part of the seventh century (Watson 1994). In the Qur'an women are told:

> and tell the believing women to lower their gaze and guard their modesty, and not to display their adornment, except that which ordinarily appears thereof; and to draw their veils over their necks and bosom, and not to reveal their adornments except to their own husbands, fathers . . . . (24: 31) (Yacub 1994: 32).

Women are also reminded that men have aggressive natures and so the Hijab is also seen as a form of protection against molestation:

> 'O Prophet, tell your wives and daughters and the believing women, that they should cast their outer garments over their persons (when out of doors): That is most convenient, that they should be known (as such) and not molested' (33: 59) (ibid.).

Veiling is seen to be a safeguard for women against men's sexual desires. Some interviewees also spoke about their schooling in Islam, which involved discussions about men and male sexuality:

> If you present yourself in a way that is not very modest then in a way you're making them cause sin of looking at you with bad intentions so if you protect yourself you protect them from sinning.
> Is this what you're taught as you're growing up?
> Yes.
> So when the teachers talk about the headscarf they also talk about what men are like?
> Yes.

For the women taking part in the study, the representation of male and female sexuality in the Qur'an and the responsibility placed upon women to manage men's sexual behaviour mean their safety talk cannot be separated out from their religious beliefs since the two are intimately connected.

At the same time, however, it appears that the act of veiling can act as a threat against western male heterosexuality, since the Hijab may reduce the potential for men to sexualise women. For some of the interviewees, wearing the Hijab has actually meant a reduction in the level of harassment experienced at the hands of men, so that in this sense the Hijab has acted as a protective cocoon. One interviewee decided to wear the Hijab at the age of 23, and immediately she noticed a difference in the ways in which men treated her:

> I think that the main argument is, in a way, you're supposed to be covering the most attractive part of the body which in the Qur'an, our holy book, it says which is the hair, wear modest clothing you know don't reveal yourself, not exposing yourself too much. So I can actually see why because I'm not saying you know, everyone should cover their hair it's entirely up to the individual but I see the differences myself. I am actually causing less attraction to people covering my hair. It's quite amazing, really, the difference. I used to get approached quite a lot before, hassled on the street by men laughing, not laughing but pointing and shouting names and all that sort of stuff. But since I've worn the veil I've not had any problems.
> Really?
> None at all, absolutely none, it's been two years. I mean even in the street when I used to walk down I used to get Asian men whistling or pointing fingers or whatever it was and I haven't had that since two years . . . . Yes definitely, Muslim men because they obviously know why, they're looking at it from a religious point of view, yeah she must be covering for this religious reason and because they follow the same religion, maybe not as practising as I am but deep inside they know yes she's doing it for that reason so we'd better not hassle her.
> What about white men?
> I've never really had a problem with white men, I used to with work men. It's quite common for them to hassle anyone but since I've worn a headscarf I haven't had a problem with them either.

It appears therefore that in some situations veiling may act as quite an effective deterrence to intimidation from men. This clearly illustrates two important aspects of veiling: veiling as a form of liberation which can prevent men from harassing women and which can reduce the capacity for the male (sexual) gaze; and veiling as incorporating social and theological expectations of how the Good Woman should behave in order to manage male sexuality, thereby implying that women are responsible for men's behaviour. It seems that the women taking part in this study have incorporated both notions into their accounts of veiling in relation to safety and protection. Of course, the women chose to wear the Hijab for religious reasons, but it seems that implicit within religious accounts of veiling are notions about male heterosexuality and its management.

In addition to examining the role of veiling in the women's safety management, the issue of whether or not the women believed that God protected them was raised. The responses provided here suggest that, whilst the women might pray to God to ask for protection, they nonetheless acknowledge that crime and violence may happen to them:

> I don't think religion really protects you in a way. I mean when we pray we do ask God to protect us. But in terms of crime to be committed against you I don't think that you can be really protected. It might happen to you one day, you don't know.

It seems that many of the women interviewed had also been the victims of a wide variety of offences, including race attacks, religious abuse, car theft, burglary and domestic violence. The study reported in this chapter took a closer look at the process of victimisation for these women, where it was found that the religion practised by them acted as a support mechanism yet, at the same time, was a focus of abuse. It seems that the acts of violence and intimidation committed against some of the women who were interviewed conveyed the message that British Muslims are 'outsiders' and 'unwanted', and seen as a threat by white territorialists and racial/religious abusers, particularly in the aftermath of the terrorist attacks in the USA on 11 September 2001.

Hate crimes against ethnic minority and religious groups

Violence against ethnic minority groups is a long-standing feature of British society (Bowling 1998). Surveys have been conducted which indicate the extent of abuse and harassment experienced. For example, according to the Newham Crime Survey, one in four of Newham's Afro-Caribbean and Asian residents had been the victims of some form of racial harassment in the previous 12 months (ibid.: 155). According to a study conducted in Plaistow, three-quarters of all victims who reported racial incidents to the police were Asian, one-fifth African or Afro-Caribbean, 3 per cent were white and 1 per cent Mediterranean (ibid.: 183). These incidents included verbal abuse, harassment, damage to property and serious physical violence. It is also important to note the persistent nature of racial victimisation, since racial harassment is likely to be a common, recurring feature of individuals belonging to ethnic minority groups. Racial crimes are also likely to be under-reported, due to the severe impact on victims (Rai and Hesse 1992).

Unfortunately, both the national and local crime surveys tend largely to bypass the issue of harassment and violence being committed against individuals as a result of the religion they follow. This means that very little information is available regarding the extent and nature of violence committed against particular religious communities. Some of the abuse and harassment experienced by Muslim women who veil has, however, been documented. It seems that veiling can sometimes arouse hostility from both the women's own communities and also wider society (Conway 1997; Franks 2000). The act of veiling adds to the 'visible difference' of Muslim women, which can intensify the extent of unfair treatment and harassment experienced (Weller *et al* 2001).

The women who took part in the study were asked whether they had ever experienced racial or religious abuse. A significant proportion indicated they had. For example, one woman said:

> Once this guy in a wheelchair starts yelling at me get out of the way and go back to your own country. I was pretty shocked by that. Paki he used . . . . I was pretty shocked, cos it was my first experience and I was like gobsmacked and I didn't really answer him back or anything like that and I just sort of stood there staring at him.

Whilst name-calling and verbal abuse might at first be considered to be merely a 'nuisance', if done often enough it can have a very severe impact on the victim. Verbal harassment and intimidation may challenge a victim's sense of security and restrict her future movement (Garnets *et al* 1992). Exclusionary language such as 'go home' or 'go back to your own country' may undermine the victim's sense of belonging. The message to the individuals here is that they are unwelcome in the social space they occupy (Rai and Hesse 1992).

Since the terrorist attacks in the USA on 11 September there have been many reports of attacks taking place against Muslim women. For example, the Chairman of the Islamic Human Rights Commission reported that an Islamic human rights campaigner has been attacked in her home on at least four occasions since the terrorist atrocities in America. She has had bricks, firecrackers and eggs thrown at her windows. Two Muslim women in Cambridge have also been reported to have had their head scarves ripped off whilst they were walking along a street. In Swindon, a young woman who was wearing a Hijab was attacked by two unknown males who repeatedly beat her around the head with a baseball bat. In Glasgow, a 20-year-old student was called 'you Muslim bastard' by a white man sitting behind her on a bus, who then went on to hit her head with a glass bottle (Sheriff 2001a). Other women have been yelled at or had guns pointed at them (Islamic Human Rights Commission 2001).

These sorts of experiences have resulted in heightened anxiety amongst some Muslim women and young Muslim girls. For example, in the *Guardian* (17 October 2001: 9) a Muslim father is quoted to have said that one of his daughters is in fear since the attacks in America: 'She wears the Hijab, she was scared to go to school, she feared being attacked.' Increased anxiety is also evidenced in that safety tips have been recently issued to Muslim women in order to try to reduce the risks of being attacked. These tips include the following: always be aware of your surroundings; travel in groups; change the route you normally travel; look confident; note 'safe houses' along your route; and tell others about your whereabouts (Siddiqui 2001). Muslim women have been informing their community leaders and the police about the harassment they have been experiencing. Despite statements made by politicians, including the Prime Minister, condemning negative stereotypes of British Muslims, it seems there has been a widespread backlash against Muslim communities.

The women taking part in this study all indicated that in the immediate aftermath of the attacks on 11 September they felt more vulnerable to harassment and becoming the victims of violence. This increased sense of vulnerability often meant that women changed their routines, avoiding places that previously they would have gone to. For example, one woman said:

> During the first few days after the attack on America my family was very cautious. My mother began to pick me up from work as I work in the city centre and when I am going home I pass by many pubs and clubs where people go to spend their evenings. My mother was also wary that the people whom I work with might also become prejudiced, but thankfully this has not happened . . . . The event has definitely changed the way my family and I move around. My mother avoided going into central town to shop until she had no choice.

This woman also turned to her faith to help her cope with her family's increased sense of vulnerability: 'I have taken it in my stride and hope that

God will protect me and my family.' Another woman said the following: 'A sensible person stays away from places where there is a potential to entice abuse.' Security around mosques has also increased since the events of 11 September: 'Our mosque committee had to hire security personnel to patrol the mosque at night. A CCTV camera is due to be installed to give 24-hour surveillance.'

One promising finding of this study is that, a few weeks after the attacks in America, some of the women indicated that their heightened feelings of insecurity had abated because they had not directly experienced any harassment or violence:

> Since the attacks on Afghanistan the situation has changed again. I don't feel vulnerable anymore, it could be due to the fact that it is now over a month since the attacks on America and nothing has happened to me or anyone I know. Plus it seems as though America has identified its enemy as Afghanistan so attention is drawn away from Muslims everywhere else.

Nonetheless, they remained wary of the impact that future political developments might have on their daily lives: 'As the "war" progresses each day is uncertain. The outcome of the previous day dictates our lives in the outside world. How safe we feel, how comfortable we feel and the growing concern of what will happen if it all goes wrong.'

Victimisation and the issue of religion: in particular, Islam

A large amount of research has been conducted into documenting the process of victimisation (Gittleson *et al* 1978; Maguire 1982; Janoff-Bulman 1983; Janoff-Bulman and Frieze 1983; Miller and Porter 1983; Shapland *et al* 1985; Mezey 1988; Lurigio and Resick 1990; Resick 1990; Stanko and Hobdell 1993; Indermaur 1995). Arising at a time when the 'victims' movement' was emerging, victimisation studies reflect an increasing attention shown towards victims of crime. These studies illustrate how different types of crime, including rape, robbery, burglary and incest, have substantial psychological, emotional, behavioural, financial and physical effects. This includes immediate effects, as well as those lingering over weeks, months and years (Stanko and Hobdell 1993). For instance, a consequence of being burgled is that individuals experience a complete loss of faith in people (Maguire 1982). Individuals experiencing violent property crime reported becoming more suspicious of people in general (Indermaur 1995). While in Kelly's (1988: 202) study of women with experiences of rape, incest or domestic violence, over 90 per cent felt that their attitudes to men had been affected by the assaults. Common emotional experiences may also be shared by victims, including shock, confusion, helplessness, anxiety, fear and depression (Gittleson *et al* 1978; Dobash and Dobash 1979; Katz and Mazur 1979; Janoff-Bulman and Frieze 1983; Shapland *et al* 1985; Brown *et al* 1990; Ehrlich 1992; Stanko and Hobdell 1993; Indermaur 1995). For instance, male victims of assault displayed shock, fear, anger and/or disbelief during the event (Stanko and Hobdell, 1993), while in Indermaur's (1995) study of victims of violent property crime the individuals experienced feelings of shock, surprise, fear or horror when initially confronted by the offender. In many cases of victimisation, individuals report a change in their behaviour. The changes can involve avoiding a specific location perceived as being potentially harmful, or can be composed of a more pervasive, general lifestyle change.

Despite the proliferation of studies about the victims of crime and the accumulation of knowledge about the process of victimisation, it appears that the issue of religion and its relationship to victimisation has largely been omitted. For individuals who practise a particular faith, there may be aspects of the process of victimisation that have not been documented by researchers and yet these may constitute an important part of their experiences. For example, might becoming a victim of crime cause a person to question his or her religion? Or in some cases, could it lead to a person reaffirming his or her beliefs? Does following Islam act as a support system to the individual in terms of providing that person with some comfort from both his or her own prayers/meditation or from the wider religious community of which he or she is a part?

A significant proportion of women who were interviewed had been the victims of a wide variety of offences, including harassment, burglary and car theft. However, it appears that an experience of victimisation did not lead these women to question their beliefs. Rather, their religious beliefs supported them in their plight. For example, one interviewee had experienced burglary on more than one occasion, which had left her feeling 'very shaken' because her 'safety net had been violated'. As well as buying a burglar alarm, her father went to the local Imam to ask for special prayers of protection: 'My dad did get from the Imam some papers with prayers on it and you stick it in certain places of the house. We also got an alarm.' Rather than the burglaries causing her family to question their faith, the crimes actually brought the family closer to Islam: 'We prayed more and asked God to protect us more. That's when my parents went into religion more.' Praying was also a strategy used by another woman: 'When these people say things to me [harassment] I just pray to myself and I don't give back. I just ignore them.'

And another interviewee argued:

> The way I look at religion, in life generally what our religion tells us
> there is good and bad. You can't have a perfect life. I can't really
> expect to sail through life without having any problems or nothing to
> happen to me, if it does I have to face it really and that's what religion
> tells us, there may be bad things there may not be. It depends on the
> individual, how God's given you your life really so I'm not going to
> turn around if something does happen to me and blame it all on God
> you know why did you do this to me? I think it's just a matter of
> dealing with the issues day by day . . . . I mean obviously we all
> need protection, we turn to Allah for protection but even if
> something bad does happen to me I can't say God you didn't help
> me.

The above quotations clearly illustrate how the centrality of faith in these
women's lives means they are able to draw upon spiritual and practical
resources to help them cope. Indeed, Islam may be helping these women
move from 'victim' status towards 'survivor' status through emphasising
the transitory nature of a crime or an injustice. Passages in the Qur'an
provide perspectives on the trials that humans can go through in life and
the opportunities for learning and growth such trials provide. In this
respect, Muslim women may not necessarily require help from agencies
such as Victim Support (Sheriff 2001b). Nonetheless, support from friends
and family may not always be forthcoming. The women taking part in the
study illustrated that in certain circumstances their local communities
were supportive, yet in other cases they were less so. One woman who had
been the victim of burglary argued: 'But in our community we probably
rely on each other for support, go to family members and stuff like that.
We live close to my dad's parents and my mum's parents aren't that far
away.'

One interviewee whose father had assaulted her mother on a number of
occasions described how her uncles would not allow her mother to
divorce her father through fear of bringing shame to the family:

> My father was quite violent. As a child I saw all of that, abusive to my
> mother. Once he attacked her so bad that she was so close to death.
> He was beating her up. My mother went to hospital and the doctor
> said that she was that close to dying. I think that he missed a serious
> vein, using a knife. She had a number of stitches, 30. I was about 6 at
> the time . . . . My uncles were saying we will not allow you to have a
> divorce. She was at the point of getting a divorce but the uncles

stepped in and said no. But my mother didn't want to take him back. Mum's brothers didn't want a divorce, cultural thing because in Islam you can divorce as a last resort. Shame if you have a divorce, shame on your family.
What does shame actually mean ?
Family honour. They can't keep their heads high.
Would members of the community criticise your mum for divorcing?
Yeah definitely, very narrow-minded community. It's the wife's fault.
Whatever he does, attacks her with a knife no it's the wife's fault.

The above quotation clearly illustrates how some women may be judged by their families and communities in terms of how closely they fit 'ideal victim' status (Christie 1986). This is perhaps unsurprising, since other research has shown that many victimised individuals may not be given victim status by their local communities, state agencies and wider society as a result of their behaviour, their race and gender, or as a result of the lifestyles they lead (Christie 1986; Elias 1990; Mawby and Walklate 1994; Lees 1997). Indeed, Henderson (1992: 105) argues that:

'Victim' suggests a non-provoking individual hit with the violence of street crime by a stranger. The image created is that of an elderly person robbed of her life savings, an innocent bystander injured or killed during a hold-up .... Victims are not prostitutes beaten senseless by pimps or clients, drug addicts mugged and robbed of their fixes, gang members killed during a feud, or offenders raped by cellmates.

The research study outlined in this chapter illustrates that women who are abused by their husbands may not necessarily be viewed as being the victims of crime. A study by Choudry (1996) on Pakistani women's experiences of domestic violence further illustrates how women may experience great pressure to make their marriages a success. Many of the women who took part in that study felt they were automatically judged to be at fault should they choose to leave a marriage. Achieving victim status for women in these sorts of situations may therefore be very difficult. It is likely that women here find support from relatively few family members/ friends.

With respect to the services provided to victims of crime by voluntary and statutory services, these have been criticised on the basis of holding damaging stereotypes of Muslim women as being oppressed and vulnerable (Sheriff 2001b). Very few agencies, it seems, have taken into account religious diversity in their practices. Social services departments, solicitors and the judiciary have been accused of not offering religious sensitivity, which may have the effect of adding further trauma to victims. The lack of funding of adequate resources also needs to be pointed out. For example, the lack of funding of shelters for Muslim women means that women who experience domestic violence are placed into secular refuges which are insensitive to their religious needs. As a result, many Muslim women decide to remain in abusive domestic environments rather than going to these refuges (ibid.).

Due to the cultural insensitivity displayed by many statutory agencies and mainstream voluntary services, the Muslim Women's helpline was established in 1990 in order to help Muslim women with problems such as divorce, domestic violence, arranged marriages, sexual abuse and incest. Since its launch, the helpline has provided a listening service, emotional support and face-to-face counselling (including the provision of Islamic spiritual counselling) to thousands of Muslim women. The helpline also receives referrals from mainstream organisations such as the police, Women's Aid and Victim Support due to the quality of care it can provide. The helpline is run by volunteers, although it does have a paid co-ordinator. So far, the helpline has not managed to secure local authority or national government funding, partly because it is a Muslim service rather than a race-based agency. This means that the helpline is run on the basis of money received either from fund-raising or from Muslim philanthropists. During the year 2000, contact was made with 3,000 women. Some 20 per cent of all the calls made to the helpline were for general information about issues such as abortion, bereavement and female circumcision, and also requests for help in finding a refuge or hostel. Marital problems consisted of 14.5 per cent of all calls, whilst forced marriages and runaway girls accounted for almost 3.5 per cent of all calls made (Muslim Women's Helpline 2001). Clearly, the helpline provides an invaluable service and, as such, should receive government funding.

Turning directly to the issue of Victim Support schemes, these offer a range of services to help the victims of crime, from providing practical and emotional support to operating witness support schemes. A study which examined the impact of a visit from Victim Support scheme volunteers found that the main objective had been to encourage the victim to express his or her feelings about the crime. Almost two-thirds of the victims said that the visits had made some difference, and 12 per cent had said they had made a 'very big difference' to how they had coped with the emotional impact of the crime. The authors of the study conclude that a group of individuals who were visited by Victim Support scheme volunteers, when matched against a group of individuals who weren't visited, tended to recover better. The visits seemed to show people that at least 'somebody cared' (Corbett and Maguire 1988). More recently, findings from the 1998 British Crime Survey reveal that of those individuals who had some contact with Victim Support, 58 per cent rated the service 'very' or 'fairly helpful' and, of those who had received visits, the proportion rose to 80 per cent (Maguire and Kynch 2000: 3). This would therefore suggest that it would be useful for an individual to seek help from Victim Support. However, some of the interviewees who took part in the study reported here argued that there might be communication barriers preventing certain women in their local communities from seeking advice from Victim Support in terms of illiteracy or being unable to speak in English:

> Did your mum go to any of the victim services?
> No because she's illiterate. Communication problem, can't read or write English because she was brought up in Pakistan. When she was young girls didn't go to school . . . . A lot of Asian women don't go to the police, some of them can't speak the language, also shame and family honour. And they have this misconception that their kids will be taken away from them.

This reflects Choudry's (1996) study in which some of the Pakistani women who had experienced domestic violence were not able to telephone for help because they could not speak English. The problem of a lack of a means of communication may further be exacerbated by the finding that there are few Victim Support volunteers who belong to ethnic minority groups. According to recent statistics released by the National Office of Victim Support, approximately 10 per cent of volunteers are from minority ethnic groups. However, in some areas where recruitment problems are particularly severe this figure is drastically lower. Moreover, findings from the 1998 British Crime Survey reveal that Victim Support schemes are less likely to contact 'black' and Asian victims than 'white' victims (although these findings must be read with care because in the 1998 British Crime Survey the number of people from ethnic minority groups was low as a result of it containing no ethnic booster sample) (Maguire and Kynch 2000: 2). Victim Support is currently trying to address race-related issues. In the aftermath of the Stephen Lawrence inquiry, Victim Support's National Council set up a working party to look at Victim Support's services. A new good practice document has been produced, entitled *Supporting Victims of Racist Crime for Local Schemes and Witness Services*, in order to try to provide effective services to victims of racist crime. Victim Support is developing a new specialist training programme for volunteers who will support victims of racist crime. Victim Support is also moving towards having a better understanding of religious minority groups. It liaises with the Muslim Women's Helpline in order to respond more positively to the Islamic identity of Muslims who have been the victims of crime (Sheriff 2001b).

Conclusion

This chapter has illustrated the importance for criminology to embrace the notions of diversity and specificity. Criminological work in the areas of both fear of crime and victimisation has often glossed over significant differences between individuals' experiences through the use of rather general categories. In particular, researchers have rarely considered the religions that are practised by the people classified as 'Asian'. However, as the study reported in this chapter has shown, religion can be a part of the everyday lives of individuals, and so may be intimately connected to the ways in which people experience crime and the ways in which they manage their personal safety.

The study presented in this chapter has shown that for the Muslim women who were interviewed, the practice of veiling is deeply rooted to the management of sexuality (in particular male sexuality) and is as such connected to the women's safety talk. One aspect of the act of veiling is that it seems to have empowered these women in public places since it has limited the extent of the male (sexual) gaze. At the same time, however, and particularly in the aftermath of the terrorist attacks in America, veiling has aroused hostility and abuse and led to attacks being committed against Muslim women. Greater attention now needs to be paid by policy-makers and statutory and voluntary agencies to the issue of religious diversity, in order to provide more adequate responses to the religious (as well as racial) harassment and abuse which is routinely experienced.

Notes

1 Criticism has been levelled at the wording of this question, the general consensus being that it fails to measure adequately fear of crime. For instance, whilst 'walking in the dark' might be a measure of fear, it cannot be a measure of fear of crime since it does not relate specifically to any sort of crime. The question is, in effect, too global, as no crime is referred to specifically and therefore very little can be gleaned from this regarding what it is that individuals do actually fear.

2 For example, I have been called abusive names by men, I have experienced physical intimidation and teenage boys have thrown stones at me.

References

Bartky, S. (1998) Foucault, femininity, and the modernisation of patriarchal power. In R. Weitz (ed.) *The Politics of Women's Bodies*. Oxford: Oxford University Press, pp. 25–45.

Bhavani, K. (1994) Tracing the contours: feminist research and feminist objectivity. In H. Afshar and M. Maynard (eds.) *The Dynamics of 'Race' and Gender*. London: Taylor & Francis, pp. 26–40.

Bowling, B. (1998) *Violent Racism, Victimisation, Policing and Social Context*. Oxford: Oxford University Press.

Brown, H. (1999) White? women: beginnings and endings?' In H. Brown *et al* (eds.) *White? Women*. York: Raw Nerve Books, pp. 1–22.

Brown, L., Christie, R. and Morris, D. (1990) *Victim Support Families of Murder Victims Project*. London: HMSO.

Choudry, S. (1996) *Pakistani Women's Experience of Domestic Violence in Great Britain. Research Findings* 43. London: HMSO.

Christie, N. (1986) The ideal victim. In E. Fattah (ed.) *From Crime Policy to Victim Policy*. London: Macmillan, pp. 1–17.

Clancy, A., Hough, M., Aust, R. and Kershaw, C. (2001) *Crime, Policing and Justice: The Experience of Ethnic Minorities. Findings from the 2000 British Crime Survey. Home Office Research Study* 223. London: HMSO.

Conway, G. (1997) *Islamophobia: A Challenge for us All*. London: The Runnymede Trust.

Corbett, C. and Maguire, M. (1988) The value and limitations of VSS. In M. Maguire and J. Pointing (eds.) *Victims of Crime: A New Deal?* Milton Keynes: Open University Press, pp. 47–59.

Dobash, R. and Dobash, R. (1979) *Violence Against Wives*. New York: The Free Press.

Dodd, V. (2001) Suspicion stalks anxious Muslims. *Guardian* 17 October.

Ehrlich, H. (1992) The ecology of anti-gay violence. In G. Herek and K. Berrill (eds.) *Hate Crimes: Confronting Violence against Lesbians and Gay Men*. London: Sage, pp. 105–11.

Elias, R. (1990) Which victim movement? The politics of victim policy. In A. Lurigio *et al* (eds.) *Victims of Crime: Problems, Policies and Programs*, London: Sage, pp. 226–50.

Eve, S. (1985) Criminal victimisation and fear of crime among the non-institutionalised elderly in the United States: a critique of the empirical research literature. *Victimology* 10: 397–408.

Fitzgerald, M. (1996) *Ethnic Minorities, Victimisation and Racial Harassment. Research Findings* 39. London: HMSO.

Fitzgerald, M. and Hale, C. (1996) *Ethnic Minorities, Victimisation and Racila Harassment: Finding from the 1988 and 1992 British Crime Surveys. Home Office Research Study* 154. London: Home Office.

Franks, M. (2000) Crossing the borders of whiteness? White Muslim women who wear the Hijab in Britain today. *Ethnic and Racial Studies* 23(5): 917–29.

Gardner, C. (1995) *Passing by Gender and Public Harassment*. Berkeley, CA: University of California Press.

Garnets, L., Herek, G. and Levy, B. (1992) Violence and victimisation of lesbians and gay men: mental health consequences. In G. Herek and K. Berrill (eds.) *Hate Crimes*. London: Sage, pp. 207–22.

Ghazal Read, J. and Bartowski, J. (2000) To veil or not to veil? A case study of identity negotiation among Muslim women in Austin, Texas. *Gender and Society* 14(3): 395–417.

Gittleson, N., Eacott, S. and Mehta, B. (1978) Victims of indecent exposure. *British Journal of Psychiatry* 132: 61–6.

Hale, C. (1992) *Fear of Crime: A Review of the Literature*. Canterbury: Canterbury Business School.

Henderson, L. (1992) The wrongs of victims' rights. In E. Fattah (ed.) *Towards a Critical Victimology*. New York: Macmillan, 100–94.

Hoff, L. (1990) *Battered Women as Survivors*. London: Routledge.

Indermaur, D. (1995) *Violent Property Crime*. NSW: The Federation Press Leichhardt.

Islamic Human Rights Commission (2001) http://www.ihrc.org/file5.htm

Janoff-Bulman, R. (1983) Criminal versus non-criminal victimisation: victims' reactions. *Victimology: An International Journal* 10(1–4): 498–511.

Janoff-Bulman, R. and Frieze, I. (1983) A theoretical perspective for understanding reactions to victimisation. *Journal of Social Issues* 39(2): 1–17.

Joly, D. (1995) *Britannia's Crescent: Making a Place for Muslims in British Society*. Aldershot: Avebury.

Katz, S. and Mazur, M. (1979) *Understanding the Rape Victim*. New York: Wiley.

Kelly, L. (1988) *Surviving Sexual Violence*. Cambridge: Polity Press.

Kelly, L., Burton, S. and Regan, L. (1994) Researching women's lives or studying women's oppression? Reflections on what constitutes feminist research. In M. Maynard and J. Purvis (eds.) *Researching Women's Lives from a Feminist Perspective*. London: Taylor & Francis, pp. 27–48.

Kershaw, C., Budd, T., Kinshott, G., Mattinson, J., Mayhew, P. and Myhill, A. (2001). *2000 British Crime Survey*. Home Office Statistical Bulletin 8/00. London: HMSO.

Lazreg, M. (1988) Feminism and difference: the perils of writing as a woman on women in Algeria. *Feminist Studies* 14(1): 81–107.

Lees, S. (1997) *Carnal Knowledge: Rape on Trial*. London: Penguin Books.

Lewis, B. and Ramazanoglu, C. (1999) Not guilty, not proud, just white: women's accounts of their whiteness. In H. Brown *et al* (eds.) *White? Women*. New York: Raw Nerve Books, pp. 23–62.

Lurigio, A. and Resick, P. (1990) Healing the psychological wounds of criminal victimisation: predicting postcrime distress and recovery. In A. Lurigio *et al* (eds.) *Victims of Crime: Problems, Policies and Programs*. London: Sage, pp. 50–68.

Macey, M. (1999) Class, gender and religious influences on changing patterns of Pakistani Muslim male violence in Bradford. *Ethnic and Racial Studies* 22(5): 845–66.

Maguire, M. (1982) *Burglary in a Dwelling: The Offence, the Offender and the Victim* London: Heinemann.

Maguire, M. and Kynch, J. (2000) *Victim Support: Findings from the 1998 British Crime Survey*. Research Findings 117. London: HMSO.

Mama, A. (1990) *The Hidden Struggle: Statutory and Voluntary Sector Responses to Violence against Black Women in the Home* London: London Race and Housing Research Unit.

Mawby, R. and Walklate, S. (1994) *Critical Victimology.* London: Sage.

Maykut, P. and Morehouse, R. (1994) *Beginning Qualitative Research: A Philosophical and Practical Guide.* London: Falmer Press.

Maynard, M. (1994) 'Race', gender and the concept of 'difference' in feminist thought. In H. Afshar and M. Maynard (eds.) *The Dynamics of 'Race' and Gender* London: Taylor & Francis, pp. 9–25.

Mezey, G. (1988) Reactions to rape: effects, counselling and the role of health professionals. In M. Maguire and J. Pointing (eds.) *Victims of Crime: A New Deal?*, Milton Keynes: Open University Press, pp. 66–73.

Miller, D. and Porter, C. (1983) Self-blame in victims of violence. *Journal of Social Issues* 39(2): 139–52.

Mohammad, R. (1999) Marginalisation, Islamism and the production of the other's 'other' *Gender, Place and Culture* 6(3): 221–40.

Muslim Women's Helpline (2001) http://www.ammet.demon.co.uk/related/mwhl/

President's Commission on Law Enforcement and Administration of Justice (1967) *The Challenge of Crime in a Free Society.* Washington, DC: US Government Printing Office.

Rai, D. and Hesse, B. (1992) Racial victimisation: an experiential analysis. In B. Hesse *et al* (eds.) *Beneath the Surface: Racial Harassment.* Aldershot: Avebury pp. 158–95.

Renzetti, R. and Lee, R. (1993) The problems of researching sensitive topics. In R. Renzetti and R. Lee (eds.) *Researching Sensitive Topics*, pp. 3–13.

Resick, P. (1990) Victims of sexual assault. In A. Lurigio *et al* (eds.) *Victims of Crime: Problems, Policies and Programs.* London: Sage, pp. 69–86.

Said, E. (1981) *Covering Islam: How the Media and the Experts Determine How We See the Rest of the World.* London: Routledge.

Shapland, J., Willmore, J. and Duff, P. (1985) *Victims in the Criminal Justice System.* Aldershot: Gower.

Sheriff, S. (2001a) Mosques fire bombed, Muslims assaulted, British Muslims under Siege. *The Muslim News* 19 October (http://www.muslimnews.co.uk/~musnews/paper/index.php?article=408).

Sheriff, S. (2001b) Presentation to the Victim Support Annual Conference, University of Warwick, 3 July.

Siddiqui, S. (2001) The Islamic Human Rights Commission (http://www.ihrc.org/file7.htm).

Stanko, E. (1985) *Intimate Intrusions: Women's Experience of Male Violence.* London: Routledge.

Stanko, E. (1997) Safety talk: conceptualising women's risk assessment as a technology of the soul. *Theoretical Criminology* 1(4): 479–99.

Stanko, E. and Hobdell, K. (1993) Assault on men. *British Journal Criminology* 33(3): 400–15.

Walklate, S. (2001) *Gender, Crime and Criminal Justice.* Cullompton: Willan.

Watson, H. (1994) Women and the veil: personal responses to global processes. In A. Ahmed and H. Donnan (eds.) *Islam, Globalisation and Postmodernity*. London: Routledge, pp. 141–59.

Weller, P., Feldman, A. and Purdam, K. (2001) *Religious Discrimination in England and Wales. Home Office Research Study* 220. London: HMSO.

Yacub, A. (1994) The woman must veil herself but not so the man. Defend the case of Islam. In *Muslim Students Scholarship Awards*. London: Fosis, the Islamic Foundation, pp. 25–58.

Chapter 4

Policing after Macpherson: some experiences of Muslim police officers

Douglas Sharp

Introduction

The police and policing are subjects of enormous interest to the general public. This is reflected in crime reporting, drama and soap opera on the television and the ever-popular detective novel. As a consequence, most people think they know something about the police. The media and the crime story generally present to the public a glorified image of policing and even the deviant cop in programmes like the *Sweeney* or the *Dirty Harry* movies is portrayed ultimately as serving the community, the ends having justified the means. The press may be more probing and, from time to time, more critical, but even here the perception must be that, for many, the police and police behaviour are not particularly problematic in today's society.

We should be, however, aware that there is no universally shared experience and this generally positive picture is in sharp contrast to the beliefs and experiences of some sections of our society. People who live in the poorer areas of our cities suffer social and economic disadvantage and people from black and Asian communities are disproportionately represented as victims of crime. Add to this the fact that people from these communities are also more likely to come into conflict with the police and to suffer negative experiences within the criminal justice system. One of the consequences of this is a perception in those communities of a police service whose policies and behaviours are informed by prejudice and racial stereotypes. Whilst it would be unfair to suggest that these views have been ignored, it is not difficult to see that the negative effects of racism have not been eradicated and it is easy to understand why some sections of our society feel alienated from the police. However, in the 1990s the climate seemed to change sharply when the Macpherson report (1999) into the murder of Stephen Lawrence brought the problem of racism in the Police Service more sharply into focus than at any other time in history.

Policing and ethnic minority groups

Until relatively recently, there was little academic interest in the police or in policing and it was not until the early 1960s that a literature began to emerge. Criticism of the police and their relationship with minority communities is not new, and the influx of West Indian immigrants in the 1950s created tensions within British society which were complicated by accusations that the police were failing to deal effectively with complaints of racist violence and intimidation. These allegations became particularly strident during the race riots in Nottingham and Notting Hill in 1958. However, this was the period which has become known as the Golden Age of policing and there was no serious academic study of the police until the 1960s. The first important published work on policing came from the USA, where early studies reported suspiciousness and hostility amongst police officers towards members of the black community (Skolnick 1966). Similar results were obtained in the first studies in England and Wales. Cain's study, conducted in the 1960s, compares urban and rural policing and describes the negative views that police officers held of members of the black community. In particular, she observed the tendency of officers to characterise Asians as devious liars (Cain 1973). Since that time the literature on police culture has grown considerably and references to race and racism abound. Perhaps the best and most relevant description is provided by Reiner who, under the title of 'Cop Culture', describes an occupational culture characterised by a sense of mission, a desire for action and excitement, an authoritarian conservatism, suspicion and cynicism. It fosters a sense of isolation and solidarity and contains a significant element of racism (Reiner 2000: 85–107). More important perhaps is Reiner's (ibid.) assertion that the police characterise black and Asian people as lower-status individuals who tend to be problematic. Further evidence of this negative stereotyping can be found elsewhere in the literature. In their important study of the Metropolitan Police, Smith and Gray (1983) noted the pervasive nature of racist language, findings which are also confirmed by Holdaway (1983). Perhaps even more worrying is Bowling's (1999) observation that, whilst they may not actually condone racism and racist violence, many police officers are prepared to admit they understand how it arises and to express some sympathy with the perpetrators.

The study presented in this chapter is, however, not primarily about race: it is about policing and the experiences of a small group of Muslim police officers. However, within the context of community and race relations in England and Wales it is extremely difficult to disentangle issues of race, culture and religion and any study must take account of the nature and role of the British police. In Britain we have taken pride in the British police model which is described as one of 'policing by consent'. The police system in this country was not designed but, rather, developed during the nineteenth and twentieth centuries and has its roots in the relationship between the police and the community. Within this context it has for long been a contention of police leaders that the Police Service in England and Wales is representative of the population they police. Indeed, it was a principle upon which Peel established the Metropolitan Police in 1829. I have argued elsewhere that in fact this never was the case (Wilson *et al* 2001) and the growth of ethnic minority populations which began in the 1950s has cast serious doubt on that assertion.

Today the relationship between police and the community is more fragile than it has been in the past and the police can no longer rely on the unconditional support of the public. The reasons for this are not difficult to find. The period since 1960 has been characterised by rapid social change and rising crime. The police have been the subject of critical scrutiny and have faced accusations of inefficiency, corrupt practices, political partiality and endemic racism. There is a very real sense in which whole sections of the public have lost faith in the ability of the service to protect them and the fear of crime is at an all time high. It would, however, be unfair to claim that the police have made no effort to become more representative and during the 1960s and 1970s small numbers of black and Asian officers did join the service. However, they only ever represented a very small proportion of the total number of officers and many left the service prematurely.

The report by Lord Scarman following the inner-city disturbances in 1980 and 1981 raised the profile of ethnic minority recruitment to the police (Scarman 1981). That report was the catalyst for a number of very significant changes in policing but, nonetheless, the progress of the service towards becoming more representative of the population has continued its slow pace. Over the last decade the proportion of recruits drawn from minority ethnic populations has increased, but the most recent figures from Her Majesty's Inspectorate of Constabulary (HMIC) indicate that only 2.2 per cent of the service is made up of officers from minority communities against about 6 per cent in the population as a whole (HMIC 2000: 3). This slow progress can be explained by two inter-related factors. First, a reluctance of people from minority communities to join the police and, secondly, the fact that ethnic minority officers are disproportionately represented in the statistics of those who leave the service prematurely. This second point is particularly problematic because it sends important messages to the community as a whole and must inevitably raise questions as to how the service can be trusted when it says it is committed to providing a fair and equitable service.

Two recently published reports commissioned by the Home Office provide clear evidence of the reluctance of minority populations to join the police and together they give some indication of the scale of the problem. Stone and Tuffin (2000), researching the attitudes of people from minority ethnic communities to a police career, give eloquent testimony to some of the problems the service faces. To quote: 'Police culture itself was felt to be at the root of many problems. The culture of the police was thought to encourage racist attitudes' (ibid.: 45). While Weller *et al* (2001: 52) in a study of religious discrimination in England and Wales note: 'Two-thirds or more of Muslim, Sikh and Hindu organisations reported unfairness both in the attitudes and behaviour of police officers, and in the practices of the Police Service.'

It is clear from these reports that there exists a strongly held belief that the Police Service embraces a culture which is at best unsympathetic to and ignorant of minority populations, and at the worst racist. In the face of the evidence it is difficult to disagree with that view.

While such allegations are not new, until recently it was commonplace to locate the problem with individual officers rather than the service as a whole. Lord Scarman (1981), for example, in his report on the Brixton riots, explicitly ruled out suggestions that the police as an organisation was racist. Post-Scarman the police introduced significant changes and began to raise the profile of ethnic minority recruitment. The police discipline code was strengthened to enable senior officers to deal more effectively with allegations of racist behaviour and new training and personnel policies were developed.

However, these have not produced the sort of improvements that were intended. The disproportionate representation of young black men in relation to the operation of police powers to stop and search suspects, a worrying number of deaths of black and Asian men in police custody and a failure to deal adequately with racist incidents combined to confirm the impression of endemic racism. In addition, a number of high-profile cases involving allegations of sexual and racial discrimination in personnel policies and practices have resulted in considerable criticism and have created a picture of unfairness based on prejudice and stereotyping. The subsequent award of significant damages against a number of police forces only serves to confirm that view.

The racist murder of Stephen Lawrence dramatically raised the profile of the debate about racism in Britain. The Macpherson report (1999) into the murder explicitly rejected the suggestion that racism was restricted to a small number of officers and accused the service as a whole of being institutionally racist. Macpherson (ibid.: para. 6.34) defines institutional racism as 'unwitting prejudice, ignorance, thoughtlessness and racist stereotyping which disadvantages minority ethnic people'. As soon as it was published the report began to have an effect with promises of revised training programmes, new policies and an increased commitment to recruit officers from minority communities backed by challenging targets set by the Home Secretary. The service now acknowledges that racism is a problem which affects not only its ability to provide a proper service to the community but also to recruit and retain minority ethnic officers. Some progress has already been made and HMIC (2000) is optimistic that the service is now showing the commitment to equality of opportunity that is necessary if it is to meet the challenge posed by the Macpherson report.

However, there is a further complicating factor, a factor which we have only recently become aware of but which is undoubtedly creating difficulties for the police. This is the problem of religious intolerance. There is, of course, a long history of mistrust and conflict between differing religions – we have only to look to Northern Ireland to understand something of the deep-rooted hostility that can divide communities – but we have only recently become aware of the problems and difficulties caused by the phenomenon known as Islamophobia. The term is relatively new having first been used in the USA in the late 1980s, but it was more recently brought to our attention in the work of the Runnymede Trust (Conway 1997: 1) which defines it as 'a dread or hatred of Islam – and therefore a fear or dislike of all or most Muslims'. It is often difficult to identify specific instances of religious intolerance and hatred. Incidents of desecration of places of worship (the temples and mosques of Hindus, Sikhs and Muslims) can all too easily be classified as racial rather than religious in origin. In fact, the original motivation of the offender may have been racist but the impact often has much greater significance for the community. In recent years Britain has become a predominantly secular society, church going and devout worship are practised by only a minority of those who nominally describe themselves as Anglicans and it is perhaps difficult to appreciate the deep offence that is caused by crime targeted at religious practice and belief. Britain claims to be a multicultural society and yet we are generally ignorant of the belief systems and practices of other cultures. We know in a general sort of way that different religions celebrate different festivals, that they worship in different ways, that their religion and culture imposes different rules regarding diet, dress and family relationships but we must question whether we really understand.

Despite the efforts of police trainers in the years since the Scarman report, there is little doubt that similar levels of ignorance exist within the Police Service. Against this background a Muslim who makes the decision to join the Police Service must then face and deal with the knowledge that he or she will become a member of an organisation which is facing the challenges posed in overcoming institutional racism but which is also largely uneducated about the basic tenets of Islam.

The present study

This study is an attempt to understand something of the experiences of a small sample of Muslim officers serving in police forces in England and Wales. It does not claim to be representative of the experiences of all Muslim officers but it does highlight some of the problems faced on a regular basis by officers whose cultural background is different from the majority of police officers. The police are not required to keep and report data on the religious affiliations of officers and we can only estimate the religious beliefs they hold. We know that most white officers would nominally at least refer to themselves as Christian and that most minority ethnic officers share a heritage from the Indian subcontinent and are most likely to be either Sikh or Muslim, but beyond that we know very little. Religion and race are not invariably linked and both Islam and Christianity draw their membership from all races and most continents; indeed, the Chairman of the recently formed Association of Muslim Police Officers in the Metropolitan Police is a white chief inspector. However, race is invariably identified as an area of concern in this study because all the officers involved happen to be from minority ethnic communities.

In making a decision to join the Police Service all potential recruits must weigh their motivation which may involve a desire to contribute to the well-being and security of society, a desire for excitement or action, a desire for job security or any combination of these and other factors against the reaction of friends and family, and against the perceptions of their own worlds as to the role and functions of the police and the culture of ordinary police officers. All recruits must do this but the pressures on those from ethnic minorities or those who hold strong religious beliefs are likely to be much more significant. We know very little about the experiences of minority officers in the Police Service. We do have some accounts which are drawn from the proceedings of employment tribunals and some anecdotal accounts from disillusioned people who have decided to leave the service but to date there is a dearth of research data on this important area.

This is a report of a piece of qualitative research which aims to illuminate some of the experiences of a sample of 14 serving police officers. It involves in-depth interviews exploring complex issues relevant to the working lives of the subjects. The interview is an invaluable tool for researchers who wish to explore areas where sensitive and deeply held beliefs and experiences are being examined. Qualitative research does not produce statistics and tables but it can yield rich insights into people's experiences, their attitudes, their motivations and their reactions.

The 14 officers who took part are not a random sample. Indeed, as there is no data on the religious beliefs of police officers, none of the recognised random sampling methods could be employed. Nor is there any claim that this sample is representative of Muslim police officers. However, whenever possible attempts have been made to triangulate the results using published reports and documentation, together with unrecorded conversations with a number of police officers of various ranks. The officers who took part were contacted using a sampling technique known as snowball sampling where 'one observed subject passes the researcher on to another, vouching for him or her and acting as a sponsor' (Foster 1996: 81). The first point of contact was an officer with just over 12 months' service who was known personally to the author. The other 13 officers ranged in service from 18 months to 16 years. Eleven were constables and two were sergeants. All are currently engaged in uniformed duties in a variety of police forces throughout England and Wales.

The interview method chosen was for a free-flowing unstructured conversation. Interviews of this nature can be problematic when analysing their content but they can also provide an extremely rich source of data. The interviews took place in locations convenient for the subjects; most were at police premises. The original intention had been for all the interviews to be tape recorded and later transcribed verbatim for analysis. However, only two of the subjects consented to this and the other 11 interviews were recorded in note form contemporaneously. All the officers involved were promised complete anonymity and no demographic information has been recorded.

What this study reveals is something of the reality of everyday life for a sample of Muslim officers serving in a variety of locations throughout the country. On the positive side, none of the officers involved voiced any deep-seated dissatisfaction or disillusionment. They voiced only a clear commitment to their chosen profession. However, these were men who were determined to make their way in the service. Others less committed or with less effective support mechanisms will no doubt have a different tale to tell. The interviews also illustrate something of the compromise the officers have had to make in order to follow their careers and some of the additional problems minority officers face in their day-to-day role.

A number of themes emerged during the course of the interviews, each of which was explored in depth. The main themes were: the central importance of religion; the importance of belonging; the pressures of policing; and the experience of racism.

The importance of religion

What is abundantly clear is the central importance that Islam plays in the lives of Muslims. We know that Muslims are likely to be more observant of the tenets of their faith than Anglicans (Modood 1997) and that finding is confirmed in this study. That in itself raises some significant questions for the Police Service and it quickly became apparent that Islam played a central role in these officers' lives:

> Being a Muslim is very important to me. . . . I am actually fasting at the moment. [It was Ramadam at the time this interview was conducted.]

> It is very important to me being a Muslim and in police terms with colleagues it has never been a problem to me.

> It's of paramount importance to me.

Although most of the officers did not describe themselves as being devout: 'I don't practise as I should, I don't go to the mosque very often and I know I am quite lax in practising my faith but I still regard it as very important, it gives me a focus.'

Another officer commented on how important his religion had been in his upbringing and how he considered it important for his own family, even though he himself did not claim to be particularly devout: 'It's something that has been drummed in through parents and has been passed down obviously through myself to my children. We are a practising religion although I can't say I am always actively practising like I should be.' In other cases officers reveal the tensions that the demands of police work can create when they conflict with religious observance:

You know my wife is more religious than I am and she thinks I should go to prayers more often than I do but you know I work shifts and it is difficult. My faith is important but I have to make choices.

My mother wants me to be more traditional with prayer and things but I have to explain to her I may not be devout but I am a Muslim inside myself, it gives me strength.

Prayer and the observance of religious festivals play a central role in the lives of most Muslims. None of the officers interviewed expressed any dissatisfaction with their immediate superiors' attitudes to religious festivals and they accepted the restrictions that police work inevitably imposes. All expressed the view that they would normally be allowed to take leave should they wish to on important festivals. Prayer was more problematic and whilst there was a general view that in most circumstances they could pray at appropriate times there were some reservations as to how acceptable that would be to some of their non-Muslim colleagues. There was also some surprise expressed that, while there were prayer rooms set aside at force headquarters, none existed in operational police stations and one officer did suggest that some festivals should have the same status as Christian celebrations:

It's not a problem this year [2000] because Ramadam is at the same time as Christmas, but I think it is a bit unfair that if I wanted leave I would normally have to take it as part of my holiday whereas for Christians Easter and Christmas are public holidays and they do not have to take annual leave. I suppose it balances out though because I can work on those days and get paid overtime and it usually does not conflict with my religion.

Others agreed that supervisors were generally sympathetic to requests to take leave for particular religious purposes and none reported situations where they had ever been refused permission: 'My sergeant is very good, he sometimes asks me about festivals and about my religion but it is never a problem to get time off if I really want it.'

Islam is clearly very important in the lives of these officers despite the fact that none of them claimed to be devout. Indeed, it is doubtful if a devout follower of any religion could easily find an accommodation between the demands of their faith and the commitment to policing. All the interviewees acknowledged that service to the public must come first and it was generally agreed that requests for facilities to attend religious activities would be received sympathetically. The only discord in tone was struck when addressing the question of prayer:

I don't think practising my religion would be a problem. If I really wanted to do my prayers at work I would not see that as a problem for me to go along and grab a prayer mat and sort of do it at work. I know that there is a prayer room set aside at HQ where people can go to pray if they wish but there is not really anywhere here. I don't think anyone would mind but I would not feel very relaxed.

And this view was confirmed by a number of others. The following was typical in tone of a range of comments:

At HQ there is a prayer room. I agree with that, there are a lot of people, not just police but civilians, who use it but I can't go there it is about 10 miles away and there is nowhere here. I couldn't just pray in the report room, I think there should be a room where I could go.

Membership of the police community

Despite the generally negative view of police culture portrayed in the literature, there are those who see it in a more supportive light. Waddington (1999), for example, asserts that the culture helps to develop a sense of *esprit de corps* and a close sense of identity, both of which are powerful features of the service. Police officers rely on their colleagues for help and advice in dealing with incidents and facing hostile and difficult confrontations. They need to know they can rely on other officers should they find themselves in situations they cannot effectively deal with on their own. That sort of trust is only developed as a result of close personal and professional relationships fostered both in the workplace and in social interactions during off-duty hours. Most (but not all) of these social networks are formed in public houses and restaurants and often, if not usually, involve alcohol. This is immediately problematic for a Muslim because Islam not only forbids the consumption of alcohol but also forbids any contact with it. As one officer put it: 'From a religious point of view people would see it as bad me just going there but from my point of view I have got to draw a band between religious and work as well as socialising.'

However, most of the officers interviewed were prepared to visit licensed premises and consume non-alcoholic drinks. Although there was also some evident tension in the decision for some of them: 'You have got to be seen to socialise and be there, and if you don't I think that's when people start thinking you're not mixing etc.' While others seem to be more relaxed and perhaps more confident in both themselves and their beliefs: 'I can't see the harm in mixing. I can't see the harm in going to premises that's licensed, okay people are there and they are drinking, fine that's up to them. My religion is that I don't and I won't.' But sometimes family members are unwilling to make compromises with their beliefs: 'My wife is more observant than I am and she will not go to anything where there is even alcohol on the tables. We don't go to social functions because there will always be drink there.'

Decisions about the consumption of alcohol are relatively straightforward and the officers generally felt they were perfectly able to choose whether or not they should take part in social activities. However, there are aspects of religious observance where the element of personal choice is constrained and, in Islam, as in many religions, one of the most significant of these relates to food. The evidence from these interviews indicates that Halal food is generally not available in operational police stations. This may not always be perceived to be a problem and officers either brought their own food or ate vegetarian options. In the words of one officer: 'I usually bring my own food in, you can't get Halal food here.' Of course that is not unusual; many police officers take packed food to work, but usually they do that because they choose to. For a Muslim there may be little choice. As one officer said: 'You can't get Halal food here but I can eat vegetarian baked potatoes, things like that, but there isn't that much choice so I often bring my own food.' Policing like much of life is full of inconsistency and the availability of food is no exception. One young officer highlighted just such a problem: 'What surprised me when I came from the Training College was that we have special food for Muslim prisoners in the cells but I can't get it in the canteen.'

When officers are working at their own police stations they can always make appropriate arrangements to eat, but that is more difficult when they are required to work away, for example, at a demonstration or a special event. On those occasions they will often be supplied with a packed meal prepared or supplied by the force catering contractor. These packed meals will usually contain meat (often pork) pies. As one of the sergeants said:

> I eat vegetarian when I'm here but when we go to public order or some other sort of event we usually get a packed lunch. They nearly always have a meat pie and it is often pork. It is very hard to find vegetarian and I have to search around and swap with the others to get things I can eat. They could easily do more vegetarian meals and I don't want to eat things that have been packed with a pork pie. It doesn't happen often that we get packed meals but there should be things that I can eat.

This is clearly an example when more thought and a little planning could avoid problems and would not be difficult. The HMIC report highlights, for example, that Lancashire Constabulary provides Halal food in its canteens, so it should not be beyond the capabilities of force catering establishments to provide appropriate packed meals. Such an obvious failure may not be the result of deliberate descrimination but it is at least insensitive, and all force catering departments can and should review their policy.

Policing

Policing is what these officers joined to do. They joined the service for a variety of reasons, as do all recruits, but many of their observations about police work and policing were really positive reflections of the attraction of police work. They confirmed the excitement inherent in police work: 'I love it, it is a job I always wanted, it gives me a real buzz. While others reported a rather more altruistic approach: 'It's great you know, you really get a picture that you are doing something useful, valuable you know.'

Some officers, nonetheless, reflected on the frustrations of police work, which were often about the inability of the police to get to the root of social problems and provide real help:

It's frustrating sometimes, when you can't really help, you can go so far but people have real problems and you can't help them.

We go to things and we can't do anything, there is no one to help some of these people.

Some officers also commented upon the sheer volume of work: 'There's never enough time, like today I'm here doing paperwork. That's just catching up, we have had some really busy days and I haven't had time but we have to get it done and it's too much really.' As another put it: 'I was on the van the other night and it never stopped, we were going from call to call all night.' Another reflected on the difference between his expectations and reality:

When I was at school I remembered this PC coming to tell us about the police, he showed us his truncheon and things but he talked about helping people. I suppose some of that was for us because we were kids but I thought it would be a bit like that. But it's not, you don't have time, the radio never stops.

Being a police officer can be stressful and dangerous That danger is derived not from the risk of injury and assault, although that is undoubtedly present, but rather a danger in the sense of uncertainty – never knowing what situations are going to be faced and what problems can arise. Police officers require support and encouragement in the same way that anyone else would, but the culture of machismo identified by Reiner (2000) as a characteristic of police culture tends to restrict the ability of officers to talk openly amongst their colleagues. As a consequence, they either suppress their emotions or rely heavily on friends and family for that support. Not everyone survives unscathed and the service suffers a high rate of marital breakdown and ill-health. Some of the problems can be magnified for officers from ethnic or religious minorities where cultural norms can exert a powerful influence on personal behaviour. It is an unfortunate fact that police culture can be inward-looking and resistant to change, and it can serve to isolate and reject rather than to include and support: 'We don't talk about it much at work, you sort of push it to the back but my family is a great support.' Sometimes that support comes in the shape of the religious community: 'They have always been very positive and encouraging to me at the mosque and in the community. I don't discuss work with them but I know I could if I wanted and that gives me support.' And: 'I am lucky I suppose, I do go to the mosque and talk about the pressures and I do get support. They are very supportive.'

But for an officer from a visible minority background there can be other problems, problems which highlight some of the tensions and stresses they face over and above the frustrations of their white colleagues. Often they highlight an unspoken suspicion that their loyalty may be suspect and whilst no one was able to give specific reasons as to why they should feel that, it was clearly an issue. One specific example of this type of tension is provided by language.

It is not unusual for people from minority communities to try to communicate with the police in the easiest way possible, and this will often involve using a minority language. This was clearly seen as a problem for officers who were concerned to demonstrate to their colleagues that they dealt fairly and impartially with all incidents. They anticipated disapproval and suspicion if they did not communicate in English. Whilst that is undesirable in itself, it also has the potential to lead to insensitive and ineffective policing. People at times of stress may communicate much more effectively in their native language and for many in the Asian community a minority language may be their first language. Attitudes of this nature only serve to create distance between police and the community at a time when they should be working together:

You know we deal with all sorts and sometimes people expect me to take their side or protect them. They will speak to me in an Asian language. I speak three languages, and they will say things like 'they will not know what we are saying' – they are referring to white officers, 'can't we sort this out' that's hard you know not because I don't know what's right and I always try to do my job properly, but because I think my mates might be suspicious because they don't understand what we are saying.

This was the experience of not one isolated officer – as another put it:

Sometimes people do try, you know speaking to me in another language but I always say 'speak English'. I want everyone to know what is being talked about. That sometimes causes anger, but it is more important to me that other officers know that everything is above board.

The final point to be made about police work is that all officers, irrespective of their race, religion or colour, are subject to the risk of unfounded allegations and often race is a convenient way of attacking the police: 'Sometimes people accuse me of being racist, more racist than white officers, they say, you're Asian you should help us – I just reply that what they have done is wrong, it is nothing to do with my race.' And while they receive some solidarity from their colleagues, that sometimes is not enough: 'It's funny, people sometimes say I am racist because I am an Asian police officer and I am supporting a white law. My mates on the job laugh and they say "but you're black, how can you be racist?" ' As another officer notes, this in itself can cause additional stress: 'They don't really understand the problems and the pressures, and there is no one in the job that I can explain it to.'

Racism

The Macpherson report established for the first time the existence of institutional racism in the Police Service, and we know that racism is one of the principal factors which discourage people from minority ethnic populations from joining the police (Stone and Tuffin 2000). It is particularly depressing to note that racially insensitive and offensive remarks are still a feature of canteen life. The situation seems to have improved on earlier years and there are indications that the impact of the Macpherson report has been to suppress the jokes and inappropriate comments, but they are still there and that is a matter of considerable concern.

This type of report was confirmed by a number of the officers with five or more years' service: 'It is different now but not so long ago there would often be jokes and comments that used language and terms that I considered to be offensive. I didn't feel that I could challenge them, but they were racist.' And another: 'Over the years yes, things have got better, people have sort of learned about religions.'

But some of the negative aspects of canteen culture still exist and racist comments are still unfortunately an element of the conversations which take place in police stations. The younger officers particularly try to ignore the racist nature of some of the exchanges and to treat it as good-humoured banter:

> You've got to get into the programme of saying I'm one of you now. I've got the same uniform on and where there's a bit of bantering we have a laugh and a joke and someone would make a comment towards me. Rather than thinking they're being racist or something against my family or my religion I'll actually throw one back at him. It's a bit of give and take.

Another officer, addressing the issue of racism, comments on the effect of the Macpherson report in suppressing racist language: 'It is definitely different now, I think some officers are afraid since the report.' However, not everyone was so positive:

> 'Obviously since the Macpherson report has come out there have been questions about institutional racism. It didn't help because people were thinking he's just going to jump on the band wagon.'

A further disappointing note relates to the quality of training in equal opportunities and community and race relations. Even before the Macpherson report the Police Service had been adopting training programmes and policies which were intended to eliminate racism. However, these initiatives are not always received with unbridled enthusiasm and there was a commonly expressed belief that the training was ineffective and could even prove counterproductive (although it was also acknowledged that such training was necessary). There is a suspicion that training in this important area is too traditional and insufficiently linked to operational police work to be effective. What seems to be happening is that police officers are increasingly learning from their Muslim colleagues. Some of the Muslim officers in this study report exchanges of information and discussions about religious and cultural practices which are informing and educating their colleagues. However, there is still a huge gulf of ignorance about other cultures and training should, and must, address that gap:

> We deal with different people every single day and it's a very important issue. Sometimes you go to people's houses not knowing. I actually walked into a Sikh house and into their prayer room with my boots on and I didn't know I wasn't supposed to. I think my colleagues thought 'You're Asian you should know these things you know but I'm Muslim and I don't know anything about other religions'.

The training these officers had received, however, failed to deal with issues both in terms of quantity: 'There is more being done now through training to try and get that awareness over, officers are being given information but it's only a small input.' And quality:

> We were given lessons in EO [equal opportunities] but they were made to be long and boring basically.

> You go over the same thing over and over, yes you have to do this, yes you can say this but you can't say that, so no one wants to pay attention even though it's a serious issue.

And there is considerable sympathy for the police trainers:

> It's not their fault really, I don't think they really know how to do this sort of training. It seems to be a lesson or a number of lessons that they have to do but they don't fit in. We all know how important it is but it doesn't seem to be real the way it's done.

The overwhelming view of these officers was that where there had been improvements in police culture they were largely brought about by the influence of minority ethnic officers rather than official policies and training. In the words of one officer: 'This is partly because of the fact that there have been incentives to recruit officers from the various ethnic backgrounds . . . . there's been a sort of general education from that point of view.' While another echoed this point: 'So through recruitment drives, etc., through people like myself and my colleague that you spoke to earlier, the awareness is getting better and people are genuinely interested in what Haj is for example.' And that sort of interest and the value of discussions about different cultures and religious practices are acknowledged by others: 'Like here I explain to people why at six o'clock in the morning we have to pray – we had this discussion three days ago with one of the Sergeants here about why we don't drink alcohol.'

Some reported what they felt to be a genuine interest amongst white officers as they are exposed to different cultures and practices: Sometimes they [other officers] ask me why I do this or why I don't do that, they are interested and they listen.' And:

> On one occasion I remember a few weeks ago we had this discussion about why we don't eat pork. Someone said it was because in the hot sun in Asian countries it went off very quickly and I said no, it was because the pig is an unclean animal. They were interested.

Some officers were able to recount very positive examples of the effect that knowledge and understanding can have: 'You know the people on my relief are very good. It's Ramadan at the moment and they even said that as I was fasting they wouldn't take their refs [refreshments] that day.

There seems to be little doubt that it is through these personal interactions that the beneficial effects described take place but, if things go wrong and inappropriate remarks are made or racism and discrimination becomes an issue, there is a reluctance to resort to official policies: 'I've never personally felt like somebody's actually been racist or prejudiced towards me, however I know that if I ever felt that, rather than going to a senior officer and making an issue of it I'd deal with it myself.'

Or because some feel that there would be further negative consequences:

> Anyway I wouldn't use them, they are about getting people into trouble and that's not the point, people need to understand. If they see people getting into trouble it just puts everyone's backs up and you get labelled a troublemaker. I would rather just confront someone who was causing me problems.

For some it is only the support of others in a similar position which enables them to continue:

> The best thing is knowing that there are others like you who experience the same things. You can like talk to them, mentioning you know and that puts things into a better view. I don't think I would carry on if I was the only Asian or the only Muslim in the force.

And despite the efforts that have been made recently and the publicity given to the assertions of senior officers that policies and practices will change, there is a depressing note of scepticism: 'You know since the report by Macpherson there have been things happening but I think they are only about being PC [politically correct]. I don't think anyone really wants to understand what the job is like for us.'

Confidential, anonymous phone lines and the various grievance procedures inspired little confidence. We should not be too surprised at this finding for, as Reiner (1991) points out in his study of chief constables, most of the people he interviewed spoke about race as a problem and in so doing often used negative stereotypes of people from minority populations.

As a police sergeant with 15 years' service recounted his early experience, one can only wonder that anyone remained in the service:

> My first day in the police was a frightening day. It was the first contact with my sergeant in 1986 – the first thing my sergeant said to me when I walked into the room was 'National Front' and he laughed. I thought oh my God what's going on here? It did worry me.

Conclusion

No job can be expected to live up to all the expectations and idealistic notions that those aspiring to them hold dear. Adaptation to a new role and lifestyle invariably involves compromise, but in a multicultural society that compromise should be a two-way process. The Police Service has undoubtedly changed, but the results of this study indicate that much of the compromise and accommodation has been made by Muslim officers rather than by the service as a whole. This finding is very similar to the conclusions drawn by Wilson (2000) and Spalek and Wilson (2001) in their studies of the experiences of Imams visiting Muslim prisoners within the English penal system.

There is of course a legitimate question as to what extent an organisation should be expected to change to accommodate the beliefs and cultural practices of staff, and there is little doubt that a really devout member of any religious group would have difficulty in accepting the restrictions and expectations a police career involves. The officers in this study do not describe themselves as devout; Islam plays an important part in their cultural identity but they are prepared to compromise and they show remarkable tolerance in the face of adverse conditions. Other less committed officers, who may be less resilient or less strong willed, do not survive. That is a tragedy for those officers. It is an indictment of the Police Service, it is a loss to the community and it adds to a perception that community policing is a slogan rather than a reality and that policing by consent has been consigned to the mythical Golden Age of policing.

Senior officers have for long been aware of the need to ensure that policing operates in ways which are not only fair and honest but which are also acknowledged to be so. Although it was undoubtedly initially slow to embrace a culture of equal opportunities, the service has made considerable strides since the passing of the Sex Discrimination Act 1972 and the Race Relations Act in 1976. All forces have equal opportunity policies, and a good deal of work has already been done to ensure that recruitment, selection for promotion and specialist posts are free from cultural, ethnic or gender bias. The progress the service has made is acknowledged in the HMIC thematic inspection report entitled *Winning the Race: Embracing Diversity* (HMIC 2000). Unfortunately, however, despite years of effort, innumerable working parties and a number of high-profile critical reports, there remains a conviction particularly within some sections of the minority ethnic community that the service has not changed or at least that it has not changed sufficiently. And the police are still failing to recruit sufficient officers from minority communities and, rather more worryingly, they are failing to retain those who do join.

Most of the problems identified by this research no doubt arise from ignorance rather than from deliberate and malicious intent. To that extent they amount to institutional discrimination and institutional racism. That is itself a tragedy because most of the points raised could be rectified with very little effort and almost no financial cost. It is surely incumbent upon the Police Service to demonstrate that commitment in actions, policies and words. There is evidence that things are moving slowly and the recent announcement by the Metropolitan Police that female officers will in future be permitted to wear the Hijab is a welcome step forward. There is no reason why that and other equally important steps cannot be taken by all police forces throughout England and Wales.

Despite the progress identified by HMIC in recruiting more police officers from the minority ethnic communities, there are still too few police officers occupying supervisory and managerial positions and the worst aspects of canteen culture are still present. They are, however, suppressed and more subtle. That in itself is a danger; any undercurrent of racism is damaging to the service and will inevitably affect the morale and commitment of younger officers whatever their background. The 14 officers who took part in this study and their colleagues from the Muslim and often minority communities face hurdles and pressures which are additional to those faced by all police officers and all those additional pressures are unnecessary. It is no surprise that officers from ethnic minorities leave the service prematurely. We should perhaps be more surprised that any of them stay.

References

Bowling, B. (1999) *Violent Racism: Victimisation, Policing and Social Context.* Oxford: Oxford University Press.

Cain, M. (1973) *Society and the Policeman's Role.* London: Routledge.

Conway, G. (1997) *Islamophobia: A Challenge for us All.* London: The Runnymede Trust.

Foster, P. (1996) Observational research. In R. Sapsford and V. Jupp (eds.) *Data Collection and Analysis.* London: Sage, pp. 81–100.

Her Majesty's Inspectorate of Constabulary (2000) *Winning the Race: Embracing Diversity.* London: HMIC.

Holdaway, S. (1983) *Inside the British Police: A Force at Work.* Oxford: Blackwell.

Macpherson, W. (1999) *The Stephen Lawrence Report.* London: HMSO.

Modood, T. (1997) *Ethnic Minorities in Britain: Diversity and Disadvantage.* London: Policy Studies Institute.

Reiner, R. (1991) *Chief Constables.* Oxford: Oxford University Press.

Reiner, R. (2000) *The Politics of the Police.* Oxford: Oxford University Press.

Scarman, Lord (1981) *The Scarman Report: The Brixton Disorders.* London: HMSO (Cm 8427; reprinted in 1982 by Penguin Books.)

Skolnick, J. (1966) *Justice without Trial.* New York: Wiley.

Smith, D. and Gray, J. (1983) *Police and People in London.* London: Policy Studies Institute.

Spalek, B. and Wilson, D. (2001) Not just visitors to prisons: the experiences of Imams who work inside the penal system. *The Howard Journal of Criminal Justice* 40(1): 3–13.

Stone, V. and Tuffin, R. (2000) *Attitudes of People from Minority Ethnic Communities towards a Career in the Police Service. Research Findings* 136. London: HMSO.

Waddington, P. (1999) Police (canteen) sub-culture: an appreciation. *British Journal of Criminology* 39(2): 286–308.

Weller, P., Feldman, A. and Purdham, K. (2001) *Religious Discrimination in England and Wales. Home Office Research Study* 220. London: HMSO.

Wilson, D. (2000) *Prison Imams – an Ethnographic Study.* London: IQRA Trust.

Wilson, D., Ashton, J. and Sharp, D. (2001) *What Everyone in Britain should Know about the Police.* London: Blackstone.

Chapter 5

Racism and religious discrimination in prison: the marginalisation of Imams in their work with prisoners

Basia Spalek and David Wilson

Introduction

A great deal of research has been generated examining the experiences that Caribbean, African and Asian people have of the criminal justice system (Hood 1992; Fitzgerald 1993; Kalunta-Crumpton, 1998). These experiences have been predominantly documented in racial or ethnic terms, placing religion as a feature of difference in a somewhat minor role (Beckford and Gilliat 1998). For example, direct and institutional racism by the police, the courts and the penal system has been discussed, yet discrimination on the grounds of religion has rarely been addressed. Nonetheless, reflecting the changing nature of British society, people from a variety of different faiths are increasingly coming into contact with the criminal justice system. It is important, therefore, to consider the extent to which criminal justice agencies have catered to the religious needs of these individuals, and the extent to which particular religions are marginalised by the criminal justice system.

This chapter examines the penal system in order to discuss how well it responds to the needs of Muslim prisoners. Christianity, in particular the Church of England, has traditionally provided religious care to prisoners. However, over the last 25 years the religious affiliations of prisoners have been changing. In particular, whilst the number of Muslim prisoners has significantly increased, those registering as Christians has steadily declined (Beckford and Gilliat, 1998). A report issued by the Runnymede

Trust stresses that Islamophobia is endemic within British society, whereby practising Muslims are often disadvantaged and discriminated against and are often the targets of abuse as a result of the religion they follow (Conway 1997). A question that arises, therefore, is to what extent do prison authorities consider and include the voices of Muslims? In other words, how well have the spiritual and practical needs of individuals who practise Islam been responded to by HM Prison service? This chapter is based upon a study which explored the experiences of a group of Imams who visit Muslim prisoners. The findings of this study suggest that, although many obstacles lie in the way of the Imams when attempting to provide religious care, the Imams have quite clearly employed extraordinary methods in order to gain greater acceptance by prison authorities, thereby improving their positions within the penal system.

Prison statistics

The religious affiliations of prisoners have changed over recent years. British prisons today are incarcerating an increasingly diverse ethnic and cultural population. Prisoners are now following a wide range of religious beliefs, including Hinduism and Buddhism and the Jewish, Muslim and Sikh faiths. According to Beckford and Gilliat (1998: 52), since 1975 prisoners registering as belonging to these religions have increased by just under 10 per cent, whilst those registering as Christian have decreased by 31 per cent. Taking a look specifically at Islam, this is currently the fastest-growing non-Christian religion in British prisons (ibid.). In 1999 approximately 4,000 prisoners were registered as Muslim in the penal system of England and Wales, sufficient to fill ten average-sized prisons (Wilson 1999).

Partly in response to these figures, the Prison Service appointed a Muslim adviser in 1999, and he has recently written that he has since 'visited over 100 establishments where I established contacts with Imams, local Muslim community groups, community leaders and Muslin prisoners' (Ahmed 2001: 19). He describes his work as being 'focussed on three main areas: Friday prayers, access to Imams and Halal diets' (ibid.). From how he describes his work, and in informal interview, the Muslim adviser seems to be adopting a managerial approach to his work, based largely on influencing Prison Service policies. His success in all this can only be measured by interpreting some of the words he uses in his writings and thus it is, for example, still a 'vision of the Muslim Advisor's office that under a multi-faith Chaplaincy the Imam will be a full member of the Chaplaincy' (ibid.: 20). Similarly, perhaps revealing the difficulties he is facing, he is still 'considering', 'advising' and 'working closely' on such issues as prayer rooms, the strip searching of Muslim prisoners and communal showers. He also admits there are difficulties in recruiting Imams due to 'ad hoc recruitment, lack of proper contracts, uncertain employment status, alongside other problems' (ibid.). Thus, it is perhaps fair to conclude that those Imams who are seeking to improve their work in ministering to the needs of Muslim prisoners are still going to have to rely on their personal skills and abilities rather than changes to penal policies.

Prison legislation

The Prison Service has a public policy statement about race relations, which is displayed in every prison:

> The Prison Service is committed to racial equality. Improper discrimination on the basis of colour, race, nationality, ethnic or national origins, or religion is unacceptable, as is any racially abusive or insulting language or behaviour on the part of any member of staff, prisoner or visitor, and neither will be tolerated (Leech 1999: 267).

Members of other religious groups have the same right to practise their faith as Christian prisoners. The Prison Act 1952 states that the prison chaplain should ensure that every prisoner is able to practise his or her faith (ibid.: 269). A *Directory and Guide on Religious Practises in HM Prison Service* has also been issued (HM Prison Service 1996) to enable staff to cater to the religious needs of prisoners more thoroughly. The directory describes matters related to worship, sacred writings, diet, dress, ministry and 'aspects of social functioning' such as the role of families, personal hygiene and race (Wilson and Sharp 1998: 19).

None the less, it can be argued that the introduction of this kind of legislation and these types of texts has not led to a significant shift in power relations between Christian and non-Christian faiths. In other words, Christianity continues to occupy a hegemonic position within the penal system. This is because in most penal institutions today, Church of England chaplains have overall responsibility for chaplaincy matters although they might liaise with Roman Catholic and Methodist chaplains. The Prison Service Chaplaincy has a statutory duty to provide prisoners with religious care, and this is run by Church of England clergy together with small numbers of Methodist church and Roman Catholic clergy (Beckford and Gilliat, 1998). This means that instances of religious and racial discrimination continue to occur, and in many prisons the providers of non-Christian religions continue to be marginalised from key decision-making processes. Instances of discrimination and abuse, amounting to a form of 'institutional racism', have been documented. In the Macpherson report (1999: s. 6034) 'institutional racism' is defined as consisting of:

> the collective failure of an organisation to provide an appropriate and professional service to people because of their colour, culture or ethnic origin. It can be seen or detected in processes, attitudes and behaviour which amount to discrimination through unwitting prejudice, ignorance, thoughtlessness and racist stereotyping which disadvantage minority ethnic people.

The study

Nine Imams were interviewed at length over several months. Whilst not a representative sample, these nine Imams worked in 22 prisons, including locals, a dispersal, male and female prisons, and young offender institutions. The Imams who were chosen for interview were randomnly selected over a period of months during training events and conferences facilitated by the IQRA Trust – a Muslim charity based in London and founded in 1987 to promote a better understanding of Islam in Britain. Working in a variety of penal settings, the Imams who were interviewed varied in terms of the amount of experience they had, ranging from a few months to as long as 12 years. Some ministered to just a handful of prisoners, whilst others might have to cope with up to 200 prisoners at prayer. Semi-structured interviews were conducted outside prison, enabling the Imams to develop themes and issues they found to be important. Each interviewee was promised anonymity, which means their names have not been included here, nor the names of the prison establishments at which they carry out their work. Some measure of triangulation was attempted by using official documentation, and facilitated by conference attendance and informal interviews with several prison race relations liaison officers and the new Muslim adviser to HM Prison Service. In particular the findings that are presented in this chapter have been further informed by an unpublished MA thesis concerning the work of an Imam who visits prisons, completed by Kashan Amar (2000).

Religious hegemony

As previously mentioned, in most prisons, overall responsibility for chaplaincy matters lies with Church of England chaplains who might closely liaise with Roman Catholic and Methodist chaplains (Beckford and Gilliat 1998). Other religions have therefore to be facilitated within prison via the prison chaplaincies. This often constitutes a site of tension and negotiation between the prison chaplains and the providers of other (non-Christian) faiths. Although the Imams taking part in this study argued that the prison chaplaincy teams are 'friendly' and 'helpful', they claimed that the structural imbalance between Christian and non-Christian religions disadvantages them and the prisoners they serve. In short there is a form of dependency. For example, one Imam revealed that:

> They [the chaplaincy team] are all welcoming. They all have a desire to do things, but I think it is mainly on goodwill rather than a commitment to do things. For example, we are asked to go in to give a two-hour lecture on finding a career and that's what it's limited to. I think the aspect of equal opportunity and the welfare of prisoners is disregarded. We are not at the moment getting involved in writing reports, pastoral care, counselling. It's all activities, teaching, lessons for the prisoners and this is all at the moment needing to be negotiated.

Many of the individuals in this study argued they are marginalised from key decisions that are made within prisons as a result of not belonging to any decision-making processes within the prison system. It seems that the majority of Imams interviewed are not members of race relations management teams, nor have they been invited to attend any race relations meetings that take place. For example, one individual said:

> I think it's a stereotype. The fact that we are not seen as a member of staff. Therefore, we are not given access to information. I am not treated as a member of the chaplain team, which I am supposed to be. Therefore, I am not invited to meetings, I am not invited to race relations meetings. I do not know when they are taking place. Most of the representation of Muslims is done through the chaplain, which is the Anglican Church. I am not allowed sufficient time to participate in events. Neither do the prison governors take advantage of the Imams in terms of informing the prison staff about Islam and Muslims within the prison system.

So, are you just used for specific events rather than involved in the life of the jail?
Yes. For rituals, information, that's it.

Another argued:

> The tangible sign would be from my point of view to involve me in the consultation processes, to involve me in being able to contribute to various forums and focus groups and also to have a continuous liaison. At the moment I find myself going into the prison as a solitary figure carrying my business in my own way. There appear to be no encounters between myself and the management.

Another Imam, also not belonging to any race relations management teams, revealed: 'I think it's an unknown area where people are unsure how much they might get involved. Obviously all the prisons are Christian dominated and a lot of effort is put into the Christian aspect of care. There are not policies as such to what a Muslim needs.'

A factor that was often mentioned which prevented the Imams from attending race relations meetings was that of time. As the Imams attend each of their prison institutions only a few hours each week, many argued there is not the opportunity to become involved in decision-making. For example, while one of the Imams was actually a member of the team in one particular prison establishment, he argued he could not attend the majority of the meetings because he was often attending a different prison on the day of the meetings: 'I am a member, but unfortunately, most of the meetings are on the same day that I am working in different prisons. It is very difficult to attend them.'

And another pointed out: 'I'd love to be, but the time I'm allowed into those establishments does not give me time to attend the meetings.'

The quotations above should cause considerable concern. Race relations management teams are responsible in ensuring that the Prison Service's race relations policies are being carried out. The teams check that prisoners are not being discriminated against in terms of access to work, education, religion and so forth (Leech 1999). It would be beneficial for Muslim prisoners to gain representation on the race relations management teams if not directly, then indirectly via their Imams. At present, however, inmates are not involved in such meetings and Imams face many obstacles to attending race relations meetings. Many Imams are employed by the prison system on a nominal/part-time basis and therefore are not integrated into the system as adequately as they should be. Prison service records reveal that the number of prisoners being classified as following an Islamic religion has been steadily rising. Between the period 1991 and

1997, the Muslim faith accounted for 86 per cent of the rise in non-Christian religions within the prison system (Annual Religious Census, Prison Service Chaplaincy, in Beckford and Gilliat 1998: 48). Nonetheless, the increase in the intake of Muslim prisoners does not seem to be reflected in the number of hours worked by the Imams. It is crucial for prisons to increase the number of hours the Imams work in order to integrate them more fully into the prison system. In this way, they might have more time to attend race relations meetings. The related issue of pay is also important since the Imams spend considerable sums of money travelling to visit their prisoners. Imams often live in urban locations, far away from the rural locations of many prisons. Prison chaplains may not wish to appoint a visiting member whose travel expenses will use up a considerable amount of their budget. Moreover, some governors limit the amount of travel expenses a visiting member can claim (Beckford and Gilliat 1998).[1] A lack of funding and support is also a problem for other religions that are practised in prison. For example, Beckford and Gilliat (ibid.) note the difficulties experienced by individuals representing the Sikh faith, who receive no Home Office funding. As a result, the treatment of Sikh prisoners is not considered to be as good as the treatment provided to Christian prisoners.

Direct and indirect racism

The issue of racism in prisons has long been a feature of academic literature (Penal Affairs Consortium 1996; Bryans and Wilson 1998; Genders and Player 1989). Racism in prison can occur directly in the form of racial harassment, abusive language, assault and so forth. Racist incidents can take place between prisoners, between prisoners and staff and between staff and other individuals visiting the prison. Racism amongst prison officers is particularly important to explore, since officers have a lot of direct contact with prisoners and visiting members as they are responsible for the security, control and day-to-day care of the inmate population (Genders and Player 1989). A research study carried out by Genders and Player (ibid.) found that prison staff held in common a number of views about the character and behaviour of ethnic minority inmates. Racial stereotypes emerged which stigmatised prisoners. More recently, Burnett and Farrell (1994: 9) have found that significantly more ethnic minority prisoners complained of racial incidents than white inmates. A third of Asians and nearly half of blacks said they had been racially victimised by staff. These incidents included assault, bullying, theft, verbal abuse and harassment. In terms of indirect discrimination, meals were found to be the most controversial area as they were seen by inmates to discriminate against ethnic minority groups. Muslim prisoners criticised the absence or dearth of Halal meat in some prisons: 'They do provide halal meat but I don't think it's true halal. It is very poor quality and it is prepared with ordinary meat dishes and served in the same dishes as other food. Islamic religion has very strict rules about diet and food preparations' (ibid.: 21). Other problems associated with practising the Muslim faith in prison included concern about the place and times of worship, or the provision of a suitable minister (ibid.).

A significant proportion of racial incidents are, however, unlikely to have been recorded or reported due to the largely hidden nature of racism in prison. Prisoners may be unwilling to talk about instances of harassment and abuse from either other prisoners or prison staff due to a fear of retaliation. Returning to the study reported in this chapter, many of the Imams who were interviewed also described that both prison staff and prisoners have behaved in a racist manner towards them. The Imams taking part in this study occupy a structurally more powerful position within the prison system than the Muslim prisoners they serve. This means their experiences of direct racism are perhaps more easy to reveal than those of the prisoners. For example, one individual explained:

Once they [prison officers] were checking the inmates and they asked us to stand in the same line as the inmates. We refused.
How did they react to that?
They didn't. They shouldn't have asked us to stand in the same line as the inmates.

Another said:

Sly remarks about Islam and Muslims, the way we pray. Names that are not polite are used. As a parson you get remarks. With Imams, myself, with Muslims it is to a greater extent. Even now it is still prevalent among certain officers. The privileges of the Muslims have been deprived.
Can you give an example of the remarks that would be used?
Oh like 'coons' 'Arabs'.

One Imam was also called racist names by the prisoners:

Some seven months ago I was shouted at through a wing by some inmates and called a Paki. I heard it once, twice, three times. It went on about ten times. I was so annoyed that I actually went into that particular wing and I stood surrounded by inmates. An officer of that wing was stood quite a few steps away from me and I stood in the middle of the inmates and said, 'Here I am. Who wants to kill me?' They all denied. They all said, 'No'. They all apologised basically, but no one took the personal flak.

The language used by individuals is quite startling, particularly when taking into consideration the fact that it is a disciplinary offence for staff or prisoners to use racially abusive language (Leech 1999).

Ignorance over the spiritual and practical aspects of Islam has led to insensitive treatment of prisoners by the prison authorities. For example, one Imam relayed the following incident to us:

I could be called a name, but I could laugh with it. When a person is disturbed when he is praying, it is through ignorance because there is an Islamic way where you go into a form of meditation where you do not turn left or right. Once you have embraced yourself you are in the presence of the Lord and nothing in the world would make you turn round. One particular incident comes to mind where an officer kept disturbing an inmate within his cell whilst he was praying. He kept coming back, kept coming back. When I approached him, he said that he thought the inmate was playing a game with him by not wanting to respond when he was calling his name. It was taken very offensively.

While another Imam argued that having to share a multi-faith room with other religions is undesirable:

Regarding the usage of the prayer room, we do have in most of the prisons, actually throughout the UK we have a multi-faith common room, now to a certain extent it is okay. But I think it is advisable, that if they allow us a separate room for Muslims to worship, then it would be more beneficial for the Imam and the inmates because sometimes we do need to stick our religious artefacts and posters and things like that. So, if we have any pictures to do with humans or something that has a life inside and it's placed on the wall which we have to face then in Islam it is not desirable, so the prayers become undesirable. I think that the government or authorities should provide us with a separate room rather than a multi-faith room. In some prisons, there is a separate room in which they can carry out their daily duties.

The findings above reflect the results of a recent Home Office Study, which indicates that organisations from most religious traditions reported unfair treatment by the prison authorities. Out of 38 Muslim organisations, 34 reported physical abuse from prison staff, as well as a lack of provision of Halal food and white favouritism (Weller *et al* 2001: 53). Moreover, thirty-four out of 38 Muslim organisations indicated unfair treatment from prison staff, compared to only 21 out of 125 Christian organisations (ibid.). In spite of the Prison Service's race relations policy, which makes it an offence to discriminate on grounds of religion, it seems that anti-Muslim sentiment, discrimination and overt racism continue to be a commonplace feature in a penal setting. Discrimination against other religions is also a commonplace feature of prison. Unfair treatment in prison has also been reported by individuals following other religions. Buddhists have argued that their chaplains are under Christian control; Hindus have accused prison authorities of ignoring their culture; Jews have experienced hostility and have criticised the lack of provision of kosher food; whilst Sikhs have argued that in prison there is a lack of knowledge about their religious customs (ibid: 53).

Improvement

Despite the many problems encountered by the Imams when visiting prisoners, the majority of those interviewed nonetheless claimed that over the years they have been visiting prisons, their working conditions have improved. For some, there has been an improvement in their access to keys and other facilities, whilst others argued there is now a greater acceptance of the Muslim faith by prison staff members and authorities. One Imam, who has been visiting prisons over the last ten years, revealed:

> In the ten years that you have been going into the jail that you go into, do you find that attitudes towards you from the staff have changed?
> Yes, it is better now than before.
> Give me examples of how it's better.
> The fact that we have the keys. That has made it easier.

Another Imam, who has been visiting prisons over the last four years, argued that:

> The tangible difference that I have been able to observe is that currently we have a better working relationship with the establish-

ment and with the management. However, my feelings are that it has taken a very long time for the establishment to come round to the idea of accepting me as a figure who is not an alien within the surroundings of the prison.

While another Imam observed:

I think prison staff are becoming more aware of Islam and Muslims, and the basic needs of Muslims. Socially, interaction has improved. This stereotyped racist attitude that I encountered in the first five years is not as prevalent, although it is still there to a certain extent. It is not as prevalent as it used to be.

The greater acceptance of Islamic religions by the prison authorities was partly attributed to the increasing numbers of Muslim prisoners. One Imam thus argued:

A gradual acceptance, which unfortunately had to be done because there are so many Muslims now who are coming into prison. I think everyone is getting worried. Even some of the staff have told me that when they first started it was unheard of, but now there are so many on a daily basis. So it's something that they have to address.

Others argued that an improved acceptance of the Muslim faith was also due to the work of other outside organisations, such as the Islamic Cultural Centre, the IQRA Trust and black awareness groups:

I think it [the improvement] was inter-personal and from work that the organisation has been doing outside the prison. Civilian organisations to improve relationships and cause awareness amongst the prison staff about the needs and aspirations of Muslims in prison. IQRA Trust, Islamic Cultural Centre, black awareness groups. These people have made a contribution.

By far the most frequent reason provided by the Imams for the greater acceptance of Islamic practices within prison was that of the role of their own actions. Interview data revealed that the Imams have actively attempted to change a negative stereotype which they believe was held by prison staff towards Muslims. Thus, one Imam who has visited prisons over the last three and a half years argued that:

I'm trying to show people more about Islam. Especially some of the officers before who may have had a bit of a negative attitude, the more they are learning about Islam they are appreciating and we are getting on better as a result of that . . . . Now, the more I am going there and they are seeing that we are open to talk and discuss, the relationships are getting more fruitful.

While another said:

I think this is probably because I have been effective in the way that I present myself; in the way that I correspond with various personnel within the prison, in the way that I represent the Muslim female prisoners, but I think that the prison has a long way to go in terms of creating the warmth and the goodwill between myself and the establishment, so that my work is recognised as a key feature within the infrastructure of the prison. I think that the recognition has to come from the hierarchy of the prison.

For one Imam, a way of gaining greater acceptance by the prison authorities was to change the way he dresses:

[I wear] western [clothing]. I like to be open-minded. When I go to prisons I don't wear a tie. I wear normal clothes, but not traditional clothes.
Do you think that's made it easier for you?
It will make it easier. If I wear different clothes I think a lot of people are not going to feel comfortable.

Traditional dress might draw unwanted attention, leading to an intensification of unfair treatment. Individuals whose faiths make them visibly different have reported increased discrimination and harassment (Weller *et al* 2001). For example, the following comments from a Hindu and a Sikh have been documented:

If you're a Hindu, you have problems. If you're a Hindu with a dot, you have more problems.

You have to let people know; you have to be strong enough not to conform – like cut your hair in order to be accepted. (ibid.: 14).

The Imam reported in this study has thus acted to reduce his visible difference in order better to fit in within the prison system.
The Imams also talked about how they have 'learned about the prison

system', and how this knowledge of 'how to work the system' has enabled them to achieve their desired goals. One Imam referred to this as 'playing the game':

> I would say that I'm a very stubborn chap. If I've wanted something, I've always exaggerated what I wanted to get the number of things that I wanted. It's having to play the game – the humble requests for certain things. The requirements were not being met, they were being passed on to the individual departments and then from the individual officer ranking right down to the inmates. I'm a very pushy character, but in a nice way. I do try to create friendships with officers and staff, and do try to meet them after work as well, just to break that ice . . . . What I actually did was, when they issued me just with the two keys to open the gates, I refused them. I said, I don't want your two keys. I want an officer with me all the time. 'We can't afford that'. Then I think it's cheaper for me to have a bunch of keys. I got them provided.

Another Imam spoke about good communication:

> It's communication. You can't get everything you need, but when you know the system and how it works you can get everything in the right way without ferreting around and pushing too much . . . . I had to find out from my own working and involvement in the prison system . . . . It's more important if you work with the chaplain, a worker, that they are positive with you. You can get a lot of things because the chaplain has got a lot of support from the prison system. Imams take time to understand the system and their rights . . . . I had to find out from my own working and involvement in the prison system.

The above quotations reveal that the Imams were not the 'passive victims' of direct and institutional racism but, rather, struggled against their material contexts in order to gain greater acceptance by the prison authorities. This clearly highlights how the Imams have often had to be resourceful and act upon the situations they have found themselves to be in in order to produce change. However, whilst their initiative has led to improvements, many Imams argued that the prison system itself must implement changes as its approach to visiting members places severe restrictions on them. For example, one Imam spoke about how he encounters difficulties when trying to gain greater time in prison: I have difficulties if I try to negotiate extra time. They say they don't have the resources, they can't afford to do this or the prisoners are at work and we cannot have access to them. It's always excuses.

It seems that the duties the Imams carry out in prison require more hours than the prisons in which they currently work allow. For example, one Imam explained that his role in prison is multifaceted and time-consuming, yet there is insufficient time to fulfil his duties and serve the Muslim prisoners in his care:

The reason is because of the restrictions of time that is allowed within the prison, the Imam is a listener, he is a preacher, he is a caterer, he is a problem-solver, he is salvation, he is family. There are so many titles that I can continue with. It is very difficult. As far as the prison is concerned, the Imam comes in and does his Friday prayers – it is thank you very much and goodbye. But it doesn't stop there. As soon as you go in, you get all the problems that the guys have faced in the previous week. One thing leads to another. There are office problems, racial abuse, the food problems, the family problems outside. Guys not being unlocked because they are unemployed, so they stay banged up. Oh, the running around is unbelievable. The time that is wasted just gathering people, chasing people up.

Another said:

It would help a lot [to be employed full time]. I've been told that it's difficult to get this full-time, but we need more hours. I need more hours to give a lot of support, a lot of the things that they need. Two to three hours in each prison *is not enough . . . .* For me it's a part-time job. I do 4 prisons for 16 hours a week. That's not enough time. We need more. I don't have the time to visit inmates in their cells to talk more about their private life, about private things, about which they don't like to talk in front of others.
Would that extra time also allow you to get more involved in the life of the prison?
Yes, I attend meetings, even some of the things the chaplains do. There are a lot of meetings that I can't attend, so I am cut off from things that are going around and happening. I have no input towards that from my side. So, I feel that I am not fulfilling my job properly. So the hours that I am doing are hardly enough to do the services, do the activities.

The Imams are therefore arguing that in order to engage in the public life of the prison to a greater degree, it is necessary for the prison authorities to increase their working hours within the prison system and to increase their pay. This would benefit the prisoners both in terms of having more quality time from the Imams for their spiritual and practical needs, and also in terms of the Imams becoming more actively involved in managerial decisions that ultimately have an impact on the lives of prisoners.

Recent research

Kashan Amar's recently completed but unpublished MA thesis, undertaken at the University of Central England in Birmingham, throws further light on to the findings we have presented above. Describing his work as a 'naturalistic case study', which involved both formal and informal interviews and participant observation, Amar – himself a Muslim – accompanied an Imam for some 14 months as he visited four prisons. The objective was to 'generate a narrative that explored the issues affecting the Imam in his role as a Visiting Minister' (Amar 2000: 27). His research is rich and detailed, and the narrative he generates would confirm the findings that have been presented above. In particular Amar concentrates on the need for better communication between the Imam and the Church of England chaplains, and the Imam's request for greater time to do his job. Indeed the Imam described feeling 'like an intruder' (ibid.: 30) in the jails he visited, and that this was partly exacerbated by the lack of communication that existed between the Imam and the chaplaincy team. The Imam – who is anonymised throughout the study, as are details of the prisons – had visited one prison for over two years, but had still not met the Church of England chaplain because Friday was the chaplain's day off! Amar concludes his thesis that the Imam's work was 'wholly dependent on the co-operation of the Chaplain, and this was often missing' (ibid.).

Conclusion

This chapter has explored the issue of religion in prisons, particularly focusing upon the experiences of both Muslim prisoners and the Imams who cater to their spiritual and practical needs. This chapter has highlighted the extent to which the penal system is orientated towards Christianity, since the Church of England clergy are primarily given responsibility to provide religious care within prison. As a result, the Imams are often marginalised from decision-making mechanisms, which ultimately impacts upon the kinds of religious care provided to Muslim prisoners. At the same time, it appears that a significant proportion of prisoners and Imams experience both direct and institutional racism and anti-Muslim sentiment. Any reduction in the level of harassment and discrimination experienced by Muslims within the prison system has largely arisen from the work of Muslim organisations as well as the direct actions of Muslims themselves. It seems that the Imams who cater to the needs of Muslim inmates have worked hard to improve their relationship with the prison authorities. It is now important for the prison authorities to remove the imbalance between Christian and non-Christian religions, granting a more equal status for non-Christian faiths such as Islam.

Notes

1 Of note, the privately operated HMP Dovegate has been the first to recruit a full-time Imam on to its staff (Ahmed 2001: 20).

References

Ahmed, M. (2001) Muslim religious provision in HM Prison Service. *The Prison Service Journal* 137: 19–21.

Amar, K. (2000) Ministers or visitors? A report examining the perceptions and experiences of a Muslim Imam in his role as a visiting minister to HM Prison Service. Unpublished MA thesis, UCE in Birmingham.

Beckford, J. and Gilliat, S. (1998) *Religion in Prison: Equal Rites in a Multi-Faith Society.* Cambridge: Cambridge University Press.

Bryans, S. and Wilson, D. (1998) *The Prison Governor: Theory and Practice.* Leyhill: Prison Service Journal.

Burnett, R. and Farrell, G. (1994) *Reported and Unreported Racial Incidents in Prisons. Occasional Paper* 14. Oxford: Centre for Criminological Research, University of Oxford.

Conway, G. (1997) *Islamophobia: A Challenge for us All.* London: The Runnymede Trust.

Fitzgerald, M. (1993) *Ethnic Minorities and the Criminal Justice System.* London: HMSO.

Genders, E. and Player, E. (1989) *Race Relations in Prisons.* Oxford: Clarendon Press.

HM Prison Service (1996) *Directory and Guide on Religious Practices in HM Prison Service.* London: HM Prison Service.

Hood, R. (1992) *Race and Sentencing.* Oxford: Clarendon Press.

Kalunta-Crompton, A. (1998) The prosecution and the defence of black defendants in drugs trials. *British Journal of Criminology* 38(4): 561–91.

Leech, M. (1999) *The Prisons Handbook* (3rd edn). Winchester: Waterside Press.

Macpherson, W. (1999) *The Stephen Lawrence Inquiry: Report of an Inquiry* London: HMSO (Cm 4262-I).

Penal Affairs Consortium (1996) *Race and Criminal Justice.* London: NACRO.

Weller, P., Feldman, A. and Purdam, K. (2001) *Religious Discrimination in England and Wales. Home Office Research Study* 220. London: HMSO.

Wilson, D. (1999) Muslims in prison. In S. el-Hassan (ed.) *Practising Islam in Prison*, London: IQRA Trust, pp. 5–12.

Wilson, D. and Sharp, D. (1998) *Visiting Prisons: A Handbook for Imams.* London: IQRA Trust.

Chapter 6

Working with Muslims in prison – the IQRA Trust

Salah el-Hassan

Introduction

This short chapter seeks to describe the work of a charity – the IQRA Trust – which aims to promote a better understanding of Islam in Britain. As such, the chapter has no greater goal than describing some of the historical milestones of IQRA and some of the work we have undertaken. Of note, the chapter describes how IQRA became involved with HM Prison Service, offering advice to that agency about the increasing numbers of Muslims being incarcerated in England and Wales, and thereafter how it sponsored research and held conferences with prison service personnel and other professionals working in the criminal justice system.

Iqra

Iqra is an Arabic word that means 'read' or 'recite'. It was the first word of the Qur'an to be revealed by God, to Prophet Muhammad (peace be upon him). *Surah* 96 (1–5) of the Qur'an begins with this revelation:

Read: In the name of thy Lord who createth,
Createth man from a clot!
Read: and thy Lord is the Most Bounteous,
Who teacheth by the pen,
teacheth man that which he knew not!

The IQRA Trust

The IQRA Trust is a Muslim educational organisation dedicated to promoting a greater understanding of Islam among Muslims and non-Muslims alike in the UK so as to promote greater mutual understanding. It also aims to encourage Muslims to participate positively and fully in all aspects of life in Britain, and to practise the teachings of their religion.

IQRA is a non-political organisation. It does not represent any group within Islam but works on behalf of the Islamic faith as a whole. Islam encourages the brotherhood of humankind and works for the peace and prosperity of all Creation. It is in this spirit that the IQRA Trust was established. With almost two million Muslims living in Britain, Islam is now the largest non-Christian religion in the country. It is important, then, that Muslims and non-Muslims in the UK gain a greater understanding of, and respect for, each other's way of life, and come to appreciate the many values they hold in common. Since it was founded in 1986, IQRA has developed a wide programme of events and publications encompassing all areas of life in Britain. Some of its earliest publications included a press-pack for journalists, suitable for inclusion in a Filofax, containing useful information about Islam. A newsletter was also published and circulated to Members of Parliament, containing some of the findings of the first IQRA research report (see below).

IQRA database essays

Most books on Islam of any academic standing are written in Arabic and other Islamic languages. Therefore, IQRA set out to build up a database of Islamic knowledge in English. Muslim scholars were commissioned to write essays on a wide range of topics covering aspects of the religion of Islam, its history and civilisation, its contributions to science and other fields of arts, philosophy and learning. Other writers were British experts in their fields. All these essays were keyed into a computer. The intention behind this project was to provide an information resource that could be accessed via computer by anyone at any level requiring information about Islam. They would provide tasters and links to more information. At present (2002) these data, covering around 200 topics, are used as a resource to answer inquiries but it is hoped eventually to make it available on the Internet via the IQRA Trust's website. Meanwhile, many of these essays have been abridged as short factfiles, and 18 of them so far have been published as leaflets and booklets in the IQRA essays series.

Research reports

Another early IQRA project was to commission a series of research reports, in the late 1980s and early 1990s, such as *Public Attitudes to Islam, Islam in LEA Schools, Facilities for Muslim Burial* and *NHS Hospital Facilities for Muslim Patients*. The latest to be published in this series is *Disaffection amongst Muslim Pupils: Exclusion and Truancy*, commissioned in the year 2000 by the National Foundation for Educational Research. This study is the first step in a new IQRA drive to study and provide for the needs of young Muslims in the UK. The need to prevent them from drifting away from Islam and into anti-social activities has become increasingly clear from IQRA's work in prisoners' welfare.

Teaching materials

IQRA is unique in providing cross-curricular teaching materials geared to the UK National Curriculum. As well as for Muslim schools, these materials are also suitable for other non-Muslim schools. Children's writers, teachers, illustrators, picture researchers and historians were commissioned to produce teaching materials on a wide range of topics. Some of these are already published and in use in schools, most recently in the form of IQRA's first *Islamic Resource Pack*. This contains most of the books, model kits, work cards, magazines, teaching packs and 'essays' printed so far. The many still unpublished teaching materials on IQRA's computer are an additional, invaluable resource in answering inquiries from teachers and pupils and recently, Muslim prisoners.

Guidance booklets

IQRA's series of guidance booklets is intended to help various groups in the community to deal with aspects of their work in relation to Muslims. The first, *Meeting the Needs of Muslim Pupils*, helps teachers understand how they can accommodate their Muslim pupils' religious requirements in a mainstream school environment. *Participating in SACREs* and *Participating in School Governing Bodies* contain guidelines for Muslim parents and teachers on how to ensure that the religious instruction their children receive meets Islamic requirements, and how they can participate in decision-making about the teaching of other subjects. Other draft guidance booklets still awaiting publication are *Meeting the Needs of Muslim Patients, Islam: a Writer's Guide, Alcohol and other Intoxicants in Islam* and *A Handbook for School Visits*. IQRA also contributed a chapter on sex education in Islam to the National Children's Bureau publication *Religion, Ethnicity and Sex Education: Exploring the Issues* (1998).

Prisoners' welfare

The guidance provided by IQRA to professional community workers included, from an early stage, work with prisons and the Prison Service. In 1992 the trust started its co-operation with the Prison Service by sending copies of the Holy Qur'an and Islamic books to prison establishments. In 1993, IQRA was asked to nominate a member of its staff to deliver an annual lecture on Islam at the Rugby Prison Service College. By 1994 the trust provided regular advice and information to the Prison Service Chaplaincy. In 1995, IQRA worked with the chaplaincy on editing the Islam section in the *Prison Service Directory* and *Guide on Religious Practices in HM Prisons*. Building on these contacts, and responding to an obvious need, the IQRA Prisoners' Welfare Directorate was set up in 1996. Its activities can be described under the following headings.

Staff training events

The first training day for visiting Imams took place in February 1997 at the University of Central England and, later that year, IQRA published a handbook for visiting Imams (*Visiting Prisons* by David Wilson and Douglas Sharp). In November 1997, IQRA held a seminar on 'Prison visiting Imams' response to the problems of Muslim inmates'. This event brought together, for the first time, over 40 prison Imams as well as other specialists. On 14 October 1998, IQRA held a network and training day at Westhill College, Birmingham, in which prison officers were trained to recognise the needs of Muslim prisoners, including those relating to Ramadan. It was attended by 23 chaplains, 24 race relations liaison officers, 12 Imams, 2 catering officers and 1 prisoner. On 9 June 1999, IQRA's fourth training event was held at Portsmouth University, entitled 'Practising Islam in Prison'. Twenty-three race relations liaison officers, 14 chaplains and 8 Imams attended the day. A book of the same title was published soon afterwards, containing the papers presented. In November 1999, a 'Ramadan open day' was organised in conjunction with the Prison Service College, Wakefield. This was an exceptional event attended by almost 270 members of staff from prisons nationwide.

Publications

These were meant to meet the needs of the three parties we serve in prisons: chaplains and officers, Imams and the Muslim prisoners. They vary from the *Handbook for Prison Imams* to the *Guidelines on the Preparation of Halal Food* and the *Who Cares?* leaflet.

Ramadan and Eid

The 'Ramadan and Eid' project was launched in 1997. It reflects the spirit of that special month. It targets prisons with a high Muslim population where dates and other special foods for Ramadan and the sweets for the Eid festival are distributed.

Other criminal justice agencies

In February 2000 IQRA Prisoners Welfare organised the first conference on 'The Muslim community and the criminal justice system' at which two government ministers gave speeches. This conference brought together many strands of the criminal justice system (from the Crown Prosecution Service and police to probation officers) to share experiences and exchange ideas. IQRA followed this up with a publication of the same title, containing transcripts of all the speeches given. In January 2001 an IQRA conference on 'The Muslim community and the Probation Service' took place. Further publications, including a guide for the Probation Service on how to deal with Muslim clients, are also awaiting publication. We also commissioned a research study on the 'Experiences of Muslim police officers' by Douglas Sharp of UCE (the findings of this research appear in Chapter 4 of this book).

Conclusion

The IQRA Trust is a small charity which has attempted to promote some broader understanding of the needs of Muslims in Britain. In this respect it has reacted to the growing awareness of the increase in the numbers of young Muslims being sent to prison, and being drawn into the criminal justice system. Throughout it has sought to work with HM Prison Service and other criminal justice agencies and, as a consequence, our training events have been held with prison service personnel, police, probation officers and others. Clearly there is a limit to what we are able to do and, given that we are not political, we have concentrated on creating a dialogue and providing information. We hope this has in turn fulfilled our broader aim of promoting a better understanding of Islam in Britain.

Chapter 7

Human rights and Muslims in Britain

Natassja Smiljanic

Introduction

As a subject for study, human rights has been somewhat neglected by the discipline of criminology. Whilst philosophers have concerned themselves with the ethics and dilemmas presented by human rights and violations of them, lawyers similarly troubled by the importance of human rights have largely tried to seek out which human rights *are* protected by law and, more radically, those which should be. There is no one definition of human rights, and legal perspectives tend to concentrate on those human rights that are set out in law or that are capable of legal protection. There is an abundance of writing on human rights from various legal perspectives, and this literature is almost impossible to quantify. There is, in fact, no general theory of human rights (Douzinas 2000: 4). Human rights as a subject of concern for criminology was first acknowledged by the Schwendingers (1975), who argued 'any crime should be defined as any behaviour that violates human rights'. Although human rights protection is conferred by the state through law, the state can act criminally by abusing those rights – and both lawyers and criminologists have concerned themselves with the state as perpetrator of crime. However, the law is also concerned with human rights as civil rights – dealt with by civil rather than criminal law. More pragmatic legal thinking is concerned with how harms to individuals can be defined as human rights and with what forms of compensation or redress are available to those who have suffered human rights violations.

In the UK, 'human rights' has tended to occupy legal discourses rather than broader social, economic and cultural ones. In fact, until the implementation of the Human Rights Act 1998, the term 'civil liberties' rather than 'human rights' was most commonly used within the British legal system. The idea of 'civil liberties' was acknowledged through common law rather than legislation, and this was the closest British citizens could get to any formally recognised human rights or, rather, as they have been described, 'negative rights' – the freedom to do whatever one likes provided it has not been prohibited by law. This situation has been fundamentally and, possibly, irrevocably changed by the passing of the Human Rights Act in 1998 which sets out specific and legally enforceable human rights taken from the European Convention on Human Rights, which the Act partially incorporates.

The passing[1] of the Act has prompted numerous discussions as to how the human rights of British citizens can be protected and enforced under this new legislation. For Muslims[2] in Britain, human rights issues are fundamental to the quality of their lives, yet a significant lack of attention has been afforded to the human rights needs and claims of Muslims. Many Muslims suffer discrimination for being Muslim in every area of life – in the workplace, in schools and in public spaces. Human rights issues also affect female and male Muslims in different ways. For example, Spalek (see Chapter 3) discusses numerous testimonies from Muslim women who have had their human rights violated in everyday life for simply wearing the Hijab.

This chapter looks at the potential for the Human Rights Act 1998 to acknowledge and protect the human rights of British Muslim citizens. In addressing such concerns, a case can be made that there is a significant gap between the somewhat idealistic notions of what human rights legislation has been set up to protect (see Klug 2000) and Muslim people's experiences of violations of their human rights. Underlying this chapter is the perspective that, currently, human rights issues are conceptualised in particularly narrow ways as exemplified by the somewhat limited protection afforded by the Human Rights Act. It is important not to assume that this relatively new legislation is doing enough to protect the human rights of Muslims; much broader commitments and policies must be developed – in cultural, social, political and economic domains – in order to furnish a truly meaningful commitment to the human rights of British Muslim citizens, regardless of religion or any other 'difference.'

A report recently produced by the Islamic Human Rights Commission (IHRC), *Anti-Muslim Discrimination and Hostility in the UK, 2000* (IHRC 2000), identified the main human rights issues regarding Muslims. Although the report loosely uses the terminology of 'human rights', the study is centred on particular cases of 'discrimination' as named and experienced by individuals and by the wider Muslim community where a specific victim may not necessarily be identifiable. In surveys conducted between 1998 and 2000, the report found that, in 2000, 45 per cent of Muslim respondents reported that either they or a member of their immediate family 'have personal experience of discrimination or hostility specifically for being a Muslim'. This figure had risen by 10 per cent from the previous year. Even more alarmingly, when looking at the gender of the respondents, the survey shows that, in 1999, 49 per cent of females reported discrimination or hostility compared with 25 per cent of males. In 2000 this rose to 52 per cent of females and 36 per cent of males (ibid.: 36).

Anti-Muslim discrimination and hostility are prevalent in all areas of British society. The IHRC reports focuses upon four major areas of concern in terms of the human rights of Muslims: education, employment, media representations of Muslims and legal discrimination. Discrimination in the sphere of education affects Muslims on a number of different levels, from exclusion due to religious requirements (prayer needs, religious dress and appearance), to religious harassment and criminal acts. Many cases of discrimination have been cited within the sphere of employment – from applying for a job to dismissal for expressing religious identity through dress and appearance, to dismissal for observing prayer times and prayer days and to, again, harassment and intimidation. Media representations of Muslims can be regarded as a fundamental problem in that they portray negative stereotypes of Muslims (particularly in relation to terrorist attacks and violence, particularly in the aftermath of the 11 September attack on New York's World Trade Center). In terms of legal discrimination, the report expressed concern that existing anti-discrimination legislation fails to take into account the problems faced by Muslims in many areas of life, in the main because such legislation deals with racial rather than religious discrimination. However, the potential importance of the Human Rights Act is acknowledged by the report, which is slightly optimistic about Muslims being able to use 'Convention rights' under the Act in an attempt to overcome the limitations of existing legislation.

The Human Rights Act 1998

The Human Rights Act 1998 introduces into British law the European Convention on Human Rights and Fundamental Freedoms (often referred to as the European Convention). This international document (which was drafted by the Council of Europe in 1950) was ratified by the UK in 1953.

Since 1966 British citizens have had the right to petition the European Court of Human Rights in Strasbourg for violations of their substantive human rights under the articles of the Convention. Despite the difficulties involved in taking a case to the European Court (mainly in terms of access, cost and length of proceedings) the availability of a 'remedy' for human rights violations has had important implications for British citizens. This is particularly so as the European Convention, unlike other comparable international human rights instruments, gives the individual an opportunity to argue their case in front of a court rather than having to rely on a human rights organisation to investigate and report on his or her behalf. Although the Human Rights Act 'brings rights home', this right of individual petition still remains if the applicant has exhausted all domestic remedies.

The Act directly 'incorporates' a number of fundamental rights and freedoms from the European Convention, which are referred to as 'Convention rights' (see Table 7.1). As well as containing the substantive 'human rights' taken from the European Convention, the Human Rights Act sets out how these rights are to be enforced. Under s. 7, an individual ('the victim') who alleges that one or more of his or her human rights (as contained in the legislation) have been violated, has the right to redress in the British courts. This can take any of the usual forms of legal redress available in Britain, such as compensation (s. 8). What is significant about

Table 7.1: Convention rights

Article	Provision
2	Right to Life
3	Prohibition of torture
4	Prohibition of slavery and forced labour
5	Right to liberty and security
6	Right to a fair trial
7	No punishment without law
8	Right to respect for private and family life
9	Freedom of thought, conscience and religion
10	Freedom of expression
11	Freedom of assembly and association
12	Right to marry
14	Prohibition of discrimination

Note: Article 13 'the right to an effective remedy' is not incorporated.

the Act is that it is only concerned with the acts of 'public bodies' or those performing a 'public function' (s. 6(3)). Hence such public bodies as schools, hospitals, universities, the police and, of course, the courts must comply with Convention rights. These bodies (as employers, as providers of health, education and policing, and as decision-makers) can all affect human rights on a variety of levels. Restricting the Act to public bodies can be regarded as a major limitation of this piece of legislation, although the case law is already growing where Convention rights have been pleaded against private organisations in addition to the common law 'civil liberties' that are already in existence.

Though not bound so to do, British courts must look to the judgments of the European Court of Human Rights for guidance (s. 2). This is particularly important as the guidelines for interpreting human rights in British case law are limited. In fact, looking to the judgments of the European Court of Human Rights is almost all that is available in terms of understanding how convention rights have been interpreted in the past since the newness of the Act means there is not as yet a substantial body of British cases. In terms of interpretation, the Act operates by stating that existing legislation must be 'read and given effect' so that it is 'compatible' with Convention rights (s. 3). If the courts do not consider existing legislation to be compatible, they can make what is known as a 'declaration of incompatibility' (s. 4), which then passes the responsibility for amending the offending legislation back to Parliament. New legislation must be compatible with the Convention rights (s. 19) and, if it is not, the minister introducing such legislation must state why.

The judgments and decisions of the European Court and the Human Rights Commission (which acted as a filter for cases before the court until 1998 when it was merged with the court), therefore, provide us with guidelines for how specific human rights issues have been interpreted. Although the Act only came into force on 2 October 2000, some interesting cases have emerged, largely concerned with the right to a fair trial (art. 6) and with privacy rights (art. 8). A Muslim seeking to use the Act in terms of arguing a case of religious discrimination would look to arts. 9 and 14, which are concerned with the right to freedom of religion and the right to freedom against discrimination (including religion).

Article 9 (freedom of religion) and Article 14 (prohibition of discrimination)

The right to religious freedom is a fundamental human right for Muslims and, under the Act, art. 9 provides potential for this right to be protected. This article states:

1. Everyone has the right to freedom of thought, conscience and religion; this right includes freedom to change his religion or belief and freedom, either alone or in community with others and in public or private, to manifest his religion or belief, in worship, teaching, practice and observance.
2. Freedom to manifest one's religion or beliefs shall be subject only to such limitations as are prescribed by law and are necessary in a democratic society in the interests of public safety, for the protection of public order, health or morals, or for the protection of the rights and freedoms of others.

No specific definition of religion or belief has been established by the European Court (Evans 2001: 51), which seems to have addressed different religions on a case-by-case basis. Islam, for example, was accepted as a religion in the case of Ahmed *v.* UK (1981), which is discussed below. The right to religious freedom is known as an 'absolute right', which means it is a right that is afforded greater protection as it cannot be limited by the courts (Moon and Allen 2000: 582). However, the freedom to 'manifest' one's religion is 'qualified', which means that, in establishing whether such a freedom to manifest is to be protected, there exist limitations which have to be balanced against this freedom. 'Manifestation' has been taken to mean such acts as practising and teaching and, as such, this may have implications for the rights and freedoms of other individuals as well as 'public safety', 'the protection of public order', 'health or morals'. Therefore a balancing exercise exists in terms of protecting the human rights of the individual wishing to manifest his or her religion or beliefs and the broader space in which this occurs.

Wadham and Mountfield (2001: 110) argue that 'in cases where discrimination because of the consequences of a religious belief have been alleged, the Strasbourg jurisprudence is extremely restrictive'. The issue of the observance of holy days in employment contexts has been a common contention and has been brought by individuals from a number of different religions. In such cases, the court has to strike a balance between the rights of individuals to religious expression and the rights of employers in terms of the contract of employment. The case of Ahmed *v.* ILEA [1977], originally heard in the Court of Appeal, was eventually taken to Strasbourg and heard by the European Human Rights Commission. The case concerned a Muslim teacher who wished to attend Friday prayers at his mosque during school hours, but his local education authority would only permit this when the 'consequences for his school were not so great', therefore he did not have a right to attend mosque every Friday under the terms of his contract of employment. Ahmed's case was taken to an industrial tribunal and eventually to the Court of Appeal, who found for the local education authority that such attendance would be in breach of his contract of employment.

In the Court of Appeal, Lord Justice Scarman's dissenting judgment (which was noted for being radical at the time – Moon and Allen 2000) stated: 'I find it impossible to say that the 45 minutes absence from class every Friday to go to the mosque constitutes a breach of this contract.' Scarman considered the effect of s. 30 of the Education Act 1944, which states that no one should be prohibited from becoming a teacher in a state school on the basis of his or her religion. He decided that the case turned upon the effect of this section on Ahmed's contract of employment and held that the court should interpret Ahmed's contract of employment more broadly. Scarman stated that a narrow interpretation of a contract of employment '. . . . would mean a Muslim, who took his religious duty seriously, could never accept employment as a full-time teacher . . . . ' He went on to consider the provisions the school could make in order to allow Muslim teachers to visit mosques on Fridays. Rather than examining the narrow nature of the contractual obligations placed upon Ahmed, Scarman examined his case from the perspective of his employment rights and, ultimately, his human rights, which he broadly considered by mention of the European Convention itself. As Ahmed was not successful in the British courts in terms of arguing he was not in breach of his contract of employment, he took up his case under the Convention and argued before the commission that his employers were in violation of art. 9. The European Commission of Human Rights, in reaching its opinion, decided the local education authority had reached a fair balance between Ahmed's religious needs and having to run the school efficiently. Such a case would now come under the Human Rights Act as art. 9 would now bind the local education authority. Similarly, employment tribunals (in considering unfair dismissal cases or other employment issues) now have to take into account the right to religious freedom in making their decisions.

A major extension to the protection of the rights of religious groups comes under art. 14, which prohibits numerous kinds of discrimination against individuals, including religion. The law has, until now, neglected the problems of religious discrimination in comparison with racial discrimination. For example, there had been no obligation on employers not to discriminate against employees in terms of religion in England, Scotland and Wales (Northern Ireland being an exception). Although the public sector has been more forthcoming in introducing religious equality into the workplace, the importance of a lack of legislation in this area cannot be underestimated. Religious discrimination is hugely problematic in terms of public order offences as incitement to religious hatred is *not* a crime, unlike racial hatred (under the Public Order Act 1986). Blasphemy laws concern themselves only with the Christian religion. Perhaps most significantly in terms of issues of criminal justice, crimes of harassment, intimidation and violence are not specifically punishable when motivated by religion only but they are when motivated by race, where higher penalties exist for harassment under the Crime and Disorder Act 1998.

Rather than using such expressions as 'religious rights' or 'freedom of religion' as encapsulated with the Human Rights Act, 'discrimination' has been the more widely used concept and, as such, it has been embodied within the legislation. However, discrimination has been couched only in relation to racial or sexual discrimination (under the Race Relations Act 1976 and the Sex Discrimination Act 1975), and this within employment contexts only: no specific prohibition against religious discrimination exists in domestic law. Similarly, those who have suffered religious discrimination have attempted to rely upon laws that protect particular racial groups – which has had particular problematic consequences for Muslims. Under British law it has been the position that it is unlawful to discriminate against a person due to his or her membership of a particular religious group, only if that religious group can be defined with reference to a 'racial group'. The meaning of 'racial group' can be found in the Race Relations Act 1976 which states: 'racial groups means a group of persons defined by reference to colour, race, nationality or ethnic or national origins . . . . ' (s. 1.1). Therefore, under subsequent case law, it has been held that Sikhs (Mandla *v.* Dowell Lee [1983]) and Jews (Seide *v.* Gillette Industries Ltd [1980]) are 'racial groups' capable of protection under this legislation, whereas Rastafarians (Crown Suppliers *v* Dawkins [1983]) and Muslims are not (J H Walker *v.* Hussain [1986])

Article 14 states:

> The enjoyment of the rights and freedoms set forth in this Convention shall be secured without discrimination on any ground such as sex, race, colour, language, religion, political or other opinion, national or social origin, association with a national minority, property, birth or other status.

The meaning of 'discrimination' under this article is unclear because of an unfortunate lack of case law. The article sets out very broad catagories of discrimination and it is likely that a case brought under this article in relation to religious discrimination against Muslims would fit into this classification without much difficulty.

Monaghan (2001: 169) has noted: 'some commentators have pointed to the limitations of Article 14 as defining its impact as marginal.' A major issue of concern surrounding art. 14 is that it is not what is known as a free standing provision. In order to rely on art. 14, in terms of arguing that a victim has suffered discrimination, this can only be done if one of the victim's other Convention rights has been affected (for example, in suffering discrimination when the right to a fair trial has been denied). A new Protocol 12 to the European Convention of Human Rights, which allows for the right against discrimination to be used on its own without reliance on any other Convention right, has yet to be incorporated into the Human Rights Act (Mowbray 2001). If art. 14 were to be free-standing, this would greatly affect the ability of victims to bring claims of discrimination under the Act.

Limitations of the Human Rights Act

Even where the law affords human rights protection, protecting human rights is fraught with difficulties. Tensions exist between human rights *claims* and human rights *protected* by the law. This very gap – between the ideal and reality – has formed the basis of much academic and legal debate. There are many limitations to the Human Rights Act – broadly that the Act only looks to the protection of what are known as 'civil and political rights,' ignoring the fundamental 'social and economic' human rights (as embodied in international human rights covenants such as the United Nations' International Economic, Social and Cultural Rights, adopted in 1966). Further, it can be argued that the Act offers little protection for Muslims who have been affected by interpersonal day-to-day violence, intimidation, harassment and other crimes – protection that is obviously fundamental to everyone's human rights. Violations of such human rights in terms of victimisation are little protected when perpetrated by individuals against other individuals. Human rights violations by a public body, which can occur in a criminal context, are, however, acknowledged – a Muslim encountering violations of his or her human rights in the criminal justice system can rely on any of the Convention rights.

The Human Rights Act is largely concerned with the human rights of citizens and their protection from violation from public bodies. However, as noted above, case law under the Act is creating extensions to these rights to those affected by organisations in the private sector. Despite this, the Human Rights Act does not protect individuals' human rights in relation to other individuals even though it can clearly be argued that when one person assaults another not only is a crime committed but also a human rights violation has take place. Generally, human rights law, as well as the Human

Rights Act, is not equipped to deal with such instances of 'interpersonal' human rights violations. Nevertheless, as individuals who are the victims of crime are not actually represented as such in a criminal justice context (where the state acts as prosecutor), there are important implications that must be addressed concerning the setting of the Act.

Through the criminal law, the state has a positive responsibility to safeguard individual human rights, and failure to provide such protection can have important implications for violations of Convention rights. Criminal attacks, violence and intimidation all affect individuals' human rights and, as specifically conceptualised under the Human Rights Act, these include the right to life, the prohibition of torture, the right to liberty and security, the right to privacy, freedom of thought, conscience and religion, the freedom of expression, and the prohibition of discrimination. Although the Human Rights Act is limited in its protection in terms of interpersonal violence and, therefore, human rights violation, the state, via the criminal justice system, has a clear obligation to protect the human rights of those affected by criminal acts. The European Court has held that even where a private individual 'is the agent of the treatment' [in this case, a 9-year-old boy was beaten by his stepfather – A *v.* UK (1998)], states must take measures to ensure that individuals are not subject to degrading treatment or punishment including such ill treatment administered by private individuals' (see Janis *et al* 2000: 122). Such a decision has important implications for all institutions involved in the criminal justice system and it will hopefully act as a precedent for human rights claims made by individuals who have been criminally assaulted or intimidated but have not had their case dealt with adequately by the police and prosecuting authorities.

Criminal attacks and limitations of the Human Rights Act

Following the destruction of the World Trade Center in New York on 11 September 2001, the number of Muslim people who have been attacked, harassed and intimidated has increased dramatically. Although no exact figures are known, the growing number of media reports of such attacks would support this observation. Muslim men, women and children have been verbally harassed or physically attacked. Muslim women in particular have been targeted: their head scarves have been pulled off their heads and they have been violently assaulted (*Guardian*, 29 September 2001). Intimidation and violence of this kind against Muslim people has tended not to be seen as 'human rights violations' and often not treated as serious criminal offences against Muslims.

Much media focus since the attack on Afghanistan has been upon conditions of imprisonment and human rights violations of a number of prisoners captured by the US forces and held at a US military base in Guantanamo Bay, Cuba. Less attention has centred on the treatment of eight (the number is still unclear) Muslim prisoners held at Belmarsh Prison in the UK under the provisions of the Anti-Terrorism, Crime and Security Act (an Act that was heavily challenged but eventually passed by Parliament at the end of 2001). Under the Act, 'foreign nationals' who are 'reasonably suspected of terrorist activities' and who cannot immediately be returned to their country of origin can be detained indefinitely without charges (this obviously includes asylum seekers). The implications of this new legislation for the infringement of the human rights of prisoners are manifold. Not only does indefinite detention violate 'inalienable' Convention rights such as the right to life (art. 2), the right to liberty and the right to security (art. 4), but it also has implications for virtually all the Convention rights that seek to protect the human rights of such prisoners – art. 5 in particular.

What is most controversial about this development in relation to the Human Rights Act is that, in order to pass this draconian piece of legislation, the Home Secretary, David Blunkett, had to 'derogate' (i.e. suspend) British obligations towards the Convention (the only country in Europe out of the 41 signatories to the Convention to have done so). In respect to art. 5 (which is concerned with the right to liberty and security and which covers cases of arbitrary arrest and detention), in order for derogation to be achieved, 'a state of emergency' must be declared. Such a declaration cannot be made through legal processes but through parliamentary approval, which was achieved in November 2001 before the passage of the Act.

It is still unclear whether the prisoners in Belmarsh are being held under the new Act, and the government has refused to confirm or deny this (*Guardian* 2 February 2002). However, it still seems to be the case that the prisoners at Belmarsh have yet to be charged. Though some media reports about their conditions of imprisonment have appeared, the terms of their detention have failed to capture public interest to the same extent as the plight of the Afghan prisoners held in Cuba. Some reports have stated that the prisoners in Belmarsh have been locked up for 22 hours and have been treated like high-security Category A prisoners. In addition, they have been denied the support of an Imam, who was suspended after the events of 11 September (*Guardian* 22 January 2002, 23 January 2002). They have also had telephone calls to their families cut off as a result of them using basic Arabic greetings, which prison warders believed to be some sort of code (*Guardian* 2 February 2002).

Islamophobia as a human rights concern

The most problematical issue in relation to analysing issues surrounding Muslims and human rights is probably the lack of information about human rights concerns and violations. A report produced by the Commission on British Muslims and Islamophobia (*Addressing the Challenge of Islamophobia*; 2001) states that 'the biggest obstacle, and an example of institutional Islamophobia, is the lack of monitoring on the basis of religion, the lack of hard information and statistics on the experiences of Muslims' (Commission on British Muslims and Islamophobia 2001: 20). 'Islamophobia' has been referred to as 'unfounded hostility towards Islam.' In practice, it has also been taken to refer to 'the practical consequences of such hostility in unfair discrimination against Muslim individuals and communities, and to the exclusion of Muslims from mainstream political and social affairs' (ibid.: 1). Although this term has been criticised, it has been argued that, due to the growth of anti-Muslim prejudice, such new terminology of this kind was required in order to attempt to encapsulate the dangers of such prejudice (ibid.).

Islamophobia can clearly be argued to be a human rights concern because manifestations of Islamophobia encompass a variety of human rights issues – from a lack of equality in the sphere of employment, to a lack of a commitment to the religious needs of school pupils, hospital patients and prisoners, to violence and intimidation directed at individuals and groups and, more broadly, to the compounding of the invisibility of the presence and identity of Muslim people and communities.

Conclusion

Muslim experiences of human rights violations have tended not to be couched in the language of human rights. In a more theoretical vein, there have been many challenges from Islamic scholars who have rejected the very notion of western human rights – a fact that provokes much concern surrounding tensions between the West and Islamic interpretations of human rights (Bielefeldt 1995; Barbieri 1999). Such analyses are beyond the scope of this chapter but they raise important issues for the practical context of human rights for Muslims in Britain. Without doubt the acknowledgement and protection of Muslim human rights have been underdeveloped – partly due to the lack (until now) of accessibility to human rights legislation and partly also due to the limited categories of discrimination. In establishing the potential for using art. 9 and 14 in particular, the Human Rights Act represents an opportunity for Muslims to have their human rights recognised. However there are major issues that need to be addressed before the law can be used positively. I have suggested that Islamophobia needs to be reconceptualised as a human rights concern so that areas of life that affect Muslims and their human rights enter into public discourse. Human rights are fundamentally a social, cultural and interpersonal phenomenon, and legal responses to violations of the human rights of Muslims are only partial remedies. The roles of policy-makers, employment and educational practices, and media responsibilities all require important reassessment in terms of attitudes towards Muslims. Discrimination, violence and harassment (as well as the invisibility of Muslim experiences) need to be redressed – and the human rights of Muslims need to find its own language as well as using what is possible under the developing legislation. To date, no major case concerning the specific human rights of Muslims has been heard under the Human Rights Act, which may already portend that the Act may be failing Muslims who are experiencing human rights violations.

The unfortunate example of the treatment of the Muslim prisoners in Belmarsh illustrates the fragility of the Muslim human rights position in Britain, not only in terms of the limitations of the protection of human rights legislation which can so easily be challenged by emergency legislation and ill-thought-out political will, but also in terms of the dangers that are evident once it can be seen just how easily human rights can be threatened and 'taken away' by the state. This and the increasing violence and harassment of Muslims have highlighted the importance of the need for the human rights of Muslims to be addressed on numerous levels. Further fear and disaffection amongst Muslim people and their communities must be avoided if we are to begin to acknowledge the serious issues bought to bear by Islamophobia and the human rights concerns it addresses. The existing tensions in how limited human rights legislation can be in terms of protecting the human rights of Muslims could threaten future possibilities of using an important discourse that itself feeds into policy and practices as well as legal responses, and that affects the promising achievements already made.

Notes

1 For background on the history of the Human Rights Act, see Parratt (1999) and Klug (2000).
2 Muslims in Britain cannot be described as homogeneous in any sense. There are

two major strands of Islamic thought, Shi'a and Sunni, the majority of Muslims practising the latter. In Britain, the term Muslim would include British-born and immigrant Muslims from many different countries and Muslims who speak different languages. See Conway (1997) for background information on the demographics and characteristics of British Muslims.

References

Barbieri, W., Group rights and the Muslim diaspora. *Human Rights Quarterly* 21(4): 907–26.

Bielefeldt, H., (1995) Muslim voices in the human rights debate. *Human Rights Quarterly* 17(4): 587–617.

Commission on British Muslims and Islamophobia (2001) *Addressing the Challenge of Islamophobia. Progress Report, 1999–2001.*

Conway, G. (1997) *Islamophobia: A Challenge for us All.* London: The Runnymede Trust.

Douzinas, C. (2000) *The End of Human Rights.* London: Hart Publishing.

Evans, C. (2001) *Freedom of Religion under the European Convention on Human Rights.* Oxford: Oxford University Press.

Gillan, A. (2002a) Muslim leader appalled by regime. *Guardian* 23 January.

Gillan, A. (2002b) Concern voiced for Muslims held in UK jail. *Guardian* 2 February.

Hegarty, A., and Siobhan, L. (eds.) (1999) *Human Rights – an Agenda for the 21st Century.* London: Cavendish.

Islamic Human Rights Commission (2000) *Anti Muslim discrimination and hostility in the UK* (http://www.ihrc.org/Islamophobia/fact-fiction.htm)

Janis, M. Richard, K. and Bradley, A. (2000) *European Human Rights Law.* Oxford University Press.

Klug, F. (2000) *Values for a Godless Age: The Story of the UK's New Bill of Rights.* London: Penguin Books.

Monaghan, K. (2001) Limitations and opportunities: a review of the likely domestic impact of Article 14 ECHR. *European Human Rights Law Review* 2: 167–80.

Moon, G., and Allen, R. (2000) Substantive rights and equal treatment in respect of religion and belief: towards a better understanding of the rights and their implications. *European Human Rights Law Review* 6: 580–602.

Mowbray, A. (2001) ECHR: the Twelfth Protocol and recent cases. *Human Rights Law Review* 1(1): 127–43.

Norton-Taylor, R. (2002) The war against terrorism is making villains of us all. *Guardian* 22 January.

Parratt, L. (1999) Unfinished business? Liberty's campaign for a Bill of Rights. In A. Hegarty and S. Learnard (eds.) *Human Rights – an Agenda for the 21st Century.* London: Cavendish, pp. 287–309.

Schwendinger, H. and Schwendinger, J. (1975) Defenders of order or guardians of human rights?' In I. Taylor *et al* (eds.) *Critical Criminology.* London: Routledge.

Wadham, J. and Mountfield, H. (2001) *The Human Rights Act 1998* Oxford: Oxford University Press.

Cases cited

National

Ahmed *v.* ILEA [1977] ICR 490.
Crown Suppliers *v.* Dawkins [1983] IRLR 517.
Mandla *v.* Dowell Lee [1983] 2 AC 548.
Seide *v.* Gillette Industries Ltd [1980] IRLR 427.
J H Walker *v.* Hussain [1986] IRLR 11.

European Court of Human Rights and the European Commission

A *v.* UK (1998) 27 EHHR 611
Ahmed *v.* UK (1981) 22 EUR COMM HR DEC & REP 27
X *v.* UK (1981) 4 EHHR 188.

Chapter 8

Conclusion: religious diversity and criminal justice policy

Basia Spalek

Introduction

This book consists of a series of short chapters each presenting a snapshot of the lives of particular Muslims living in Britain in terms of their experiences of crime and the criminal justice system. The underpinning rationale for this book has been to introduce greater diversity and specificity into criminological accounts of a diverse range of issues, including victimisation, fear of crime, causes of crime and penal policy. Embedded within the different authors' contributions are observations about what new knowledge can be gleaned from focusing upon the often-marginalised issue of religion and placing it at the centre of criminological analysis. The religion that has been explored is Islam, the justification for this being that Islam is practised by a significant number of people living in Britain and that it is very much a central part of these individuals' everyday lives. The contributions in this book raise a number of important issues, and it is worth reiterating some of these here.

Modernity, postmodernity and knowledge claims

The discipline of criminology, alongside other social sciences, emerged during the 'modern' era. Walklate (2001) argues that this has meant that traditional conceptions of science have been followed, which have inevitably imposed constraints on the development of knowledge. As a result, there has been an 'implicit acceptance of a view of the world which equated human experience with male experience' (Walklate 2001: 178). I would suggest that a further significant constraint on knowledge has been that of the silencing of religious experiences and perceptions. As it is not possible to place faith into a framework that seeks to be rational and objective, this means that criminological investigations have often bypassed the spiritual underpinnings of people's lives. This can be seen most clearly when we look at the general area of 'race and crime', whereby human experience has often been equated with ethnic identity rather than religious affiliation. The widespread use of quantitative surveys has helped to skew our knowledge of social experience through the lens of 'ethnic identity' rather than 'religious identity' because both national and local crime surveys have usually used ethnic categories when classifying people. As a result, particular experiences which relate to the religions that individuals practise have been largely ignored. The issue of self-identity appears to be crucial here because surveys require respondents to identify themselves with a prearranged classification without exploring the extent to which the respondents view themselves as belonging to any of those constructed categories. Where the match between category and self-identity is weak, this will have the effect of glossing over important aspects of a person's life. This is what appears to have happened in the case of British Muslims. Researchers have often grouped people according to their ethnic identity rather than their religious affiliation even though, for many Muslims, Islam is the single, most important part of their self-identity. Although individuals' Islamic beliefs and practices are no doubt influenced by their cultures and countries of origin, this should not divert our attention from religious practices and beliefs and their role in social life. A significant number of Muslims would define their experiences through the lens of religion rather than race, or at least religious identity might be viewed by a significant proportion of them as being as important as that of their ethnic identity.

This book, then, is a reaction against the universalistic assumptions often made with respect to ethnic minority groups. The people portrayed in this book, who are mostly of Bangladeshi, Pakistani and Indian origin, have been viewed predominantly as Muslims, and questions have been asked about their experiences of crime as Muslims. In this way, the research studies presented in the book are based around the participants' own views of themselves rather than the researchers imposing categories and definitions upon them:

> [These views argue for] a relativistic stance towards knowledge and the knowledge construction process rather than a universalistic

stance. And whilst many criminologists and victimologists might recognise the difficulties inherent in a universalistic position, they equally resist the move towards acknowledging the relativism in much of the work that they do (Walklate 2001: 182).

In constructing knowledge that directly comes from people's own definitions and interpretations, new avenues of analysis are opened. To illustrate this point, the area of fear of crime can be used as an example here. It is astonishing that, despite the huge amount of research which has been carried out into fear of crime and the significant contribution made by feminists, crime-related anxiety amongst religious communities whose religious requirements make them visibly different has not been documented. For Muslim women, wearing the Hijab may reduce the potential for men to sexualise and harass them. At the same time, however, and particularly in the light of the terrorist attacks in America, the Hijab may provoke violence and abuse. This illustrates the need for fresh material to be injected into traditional criminological debates, material which arises from research that is directed at hitherto forgotten communities. Through focusing upon the lives of some British Muslims, some new perspectives and questions have been generated by this book, particularly in the areas discussed below.

Victimisation and religion

The research presented in this book illustrates that, for people who are religious, their faith can be an important source of help in terms of enabling them to come to terms with the physical, emotional and psychological impacts of crime. With respect to Islam, this is a resource Muslim victims often draw upon when confronted by crime. It may be the case that these individuals cope better with the adverse effects of some types of crime as a result of using the spiritual and material guidance provided by the Qur'an and hadiths. At the same time, following Islam places a person within a wider community that can also act as a support mechanism. This may mean that, in some instances of victimisation, traditional victim services such as Victim Support schemes may not be needed. This is particularly relevant to street crime and burglary, since achieving victim status is easier than in cases of sexual crime and domestic violence. With respect to the latter types of crime, previous research has shown that victims may be judged negatively by their wider communities and divorce or separation may be strongly discouraged and prevented within Muslim families. This means that it is particularly important for responses to women's victimisation to provide not only practical and emotional help but also religious and spiritual support. Diversity amongst women has often been viewed in terms of race or class, so that responses to women's victimisation have often failed to take into account their spiritual needs. Women's refuges have been criticised by Muslim women for failing to take their religion into account. It seems that some victim initiatives have incorporated a mistaken belief that Islam represses women and as such Muslim women should be 'freed' of their faith. This view is contested by many Muslim women who are committed to their religious beliefs and practices. This is why it is crucial to expand services that are particularly aimed at Muslim victims of incest, sexual assault and domestic violence, since these are underfunded and few in number. Secular-based support systems are not likely to adequately address the needs of Muslim victims, which is why systems that incorporate religious diversity in general, and Islam in particular, must be developed.

An understanding of hate crime on the basis of religion as well as race should also be more fully incorporated within responses to victimisation. Individuals who practise religions that require followers to be visibly different are particularly vulnerable to religious-based harassment and abuse. Muslim women who wear the Hijab have sometimes found themselves to be the targets of violence. It is important to document these experiences and to explore the consequences of such attacks upon the victims. At the same time, it is important to address crime-related anxiety amongst Muslim communities since religious-based harassment is likely to have a severe impact upon Muslims' fear of crime and their crime-avoidance strategies. As a result of the backlash against Muslim communities in the aftermath of the terrorist attacks in America, some Muslims (particularly women) severely curtailed their day-to-day activities. Whilst wearing the Hijab might be a way of managing male sexuality, in the aftermath of the events of 11 September, the Hijab increased some women's sense of vulnerability as this could draw unwanted attention and possible violence.

Criminal justice responses to religious diversity

The lack of sensitivity shown to religious issues amongst many victim initiatives is reflected throughout the criminal justice system. Agencies such as the police, the Probation Service and the Prison Service have rarely focused upon responding to religious diversity. Mission statements and policy documents may superficially refer to catering to the religious needs of both victims and offenders or to responding to religious hate crime but, in practice, these have rarely led to significant improvements for individuals belonging to religious minority groups. The penal system provides a typical example of this, since even though the members of other religious groups have the same right to practise their faith as Christian prisoners, in practice non-Christian faiths are disadvantaged as a result of them occupying a structurally less powerful position. This is because in most penal institutions, Church of England chaplains have overall responsibility for chaplaincy matters (Beckford and Gilliat 1998). Muslim prisoners, together with the Imams who provide their spiritual and pastoral care, have criticised prisons for the lack of Halal food, for the lack of adequate prayer facilities and for the marginalisation of Muslim perspectives from key decision-making processes. Working within the criminal justice system and belonging to a religious minority group can also be problematic for the individuals concerned. Muslim police officers, for example, have argued that the problems they experience as a result of belonging to an ethnic minority group in a service that is institutionally racist are often compounded by the fact that they also belong to a religious minority group. It seems that any improved understanding of Islam within police forces has arisen largely out of the daily interactions between Muslim and non-Muslim police officers rather than any specific policy initiatives or equal opportunities schemes. This suggests that the Police Service itself still needs to do more to grapple with issues of diversity and difference and needs to re-examine the structure and content of training programmes.

Religion, subcultures and crime

Another message to take from this book is that increased sensitivity to religion may also lead to developing a greater understanding of why particular individuals from particular communities engage in criminal and anti-social behaviour. Thus it is important to view young Asian men not only from an ethnic perspective but also from a religious one when examining their offending. Further research of the lives and subcultures of young Asian men is now needed, specifically looking at the issue of religion and its connections to crime. Prison statistics of the number of Sikh, Hindu and Muslim prisoners seem to suggest that Muslim offenders are over-represented in the prison population. This means that it is crucial we explore the socioeconomic, cultural and religious dimensions to their offending behaviour. Social exclusion, segregation and racism clearly play a role, but it is also important to explore the various subcultures these men belong to and the social and moral codes they live by. In certain cases, some of the men may have developed extremist views of Islam, which incorporate anti-western attitudes and which act as justifications for a range of aggressive and violent behaviours. When looking at the minority of young Muslim men who commit crime, interpretations of Islam, as well as the influence from Islamist (extremist) groups, may therefore be particularly salient. Physical acts of violence against women and gay and lesbian communities have been noted; in some situations some men have been known to police women's movements and to monitor their dress codes. Where religion is used as a way of justifying violent behaviour, it may be particularly difficult to prevent or control it. The men who engage in these activities are also likely to have a significant distrust of the police. In pointing out these factors, there is a risk of being accused of being anti-Islamic; however, I would argue that it is only through discussing these issues that we can come to understand better the lives and experiences of young Muslim men, particularly of the minority who commit crime. However, this does not mean there are any straightforward solutions. Following Islam may provide individuals with particular perspectives and lifestyles, which sometimes may well conflict with criminal justice and legal processes and interpretations. Although the Human Rights Act 1998 incorporates the right to religious freedom, this freedom is restricted according to issues of 'public safety', 'public order' and 'health and morality'. As a result, an individual may not always be able fully to manifest his or her religious beliefs, since the wider public space they occupy imposes limits.

This then raises the issue of the extent to which it would be possible, or advantageous, to deal with conflicts that affect Muslims in a culturally more sensitive manner. A related point here is the extent to which British Muslims should have control over responses to any criminal activity that takes place within their own communities. The issue of implementing Sharia law generates many questions and controversies which are beyond the scope of this book. Clearly tensions between state law and community custom will arise, as mentioned above. Nevertheless, it might be argued that it would be beneficial to gain a greater involvement of Muslim communities in crime-related matters. Rather than Muslim offenders being processed by an unemotional, distant, criminal justice system that does not have a very good understanding of Islam, restorative justice might be a way of involving Muslim perspectives in responses to crime and victimisation. Some restorative justice initiatives, as well as including the offender and victim (and their respective families), also incorporate a whole array of community representatives who come together to discuss the offence that has been committed, its impact on the victim(s) and to decide upon a valid response to that crime. In this way, it is argued that communities can take responsibility for the control of crime in their neighbourhoods and develop better responses to both victims and offenders (Johnstone 2002).[1] Through adopting restorative justice principles and practices, Muslim communities could have a greater control over the offences that occur in their own communities, and a better way of responding to Muslim offenders could be developed, one which acknowledges their faith. Recently, governments in the western world have increased their interest in restorative justice, although the extent to which restorative justice models will be incorporated into criminal justice systems, or the extent to which they will radically change criminal justice approaches to offending, is as yet unknown (ibid.). The significance of restorative justice in the context of this book is that it may enable a more sensitive approach to Muslim communities and their problems with crime to be developed.

Conclusion

Within an increasingly multicultural society, it is of paramount importance that aspects of difference that have been hitherto largely forgotten are explored and addressed. One aspect of difference looked at in this book is that of religion. Through examining the lives of some people who practise Islam, it has been demonstrated that for individuals whose faith constitutes a fundamental part of their lives, religious beliefs and practices cannot be separated out from experiences of crime and the criminal justice system. As such, it is important that policy-makers and state agencies now take the issue of religious diversity more seriously and, certainly, much more research needs to be carried out with individuals from a range of different faiths. In this way, more effective policies on crime and victimisation can be implemented – policies that more specifically cater to the needs of specific communities.

Notes

1   The question of whether restorative justice programmes will work in modern societies that consist of more fragmented communities is contentious (see Johnstone 2002). Where community links are weak, and where communities have insufficient resources to put together an effective response to crime, implementing restorative justice initiatives may be particularly problematic.

References

Beckford, J. and Gilliat, S. (1998) *Religion in Prison: Equal Rites in a Multi-Faith Society*. Cambridge: Cambridge University Press.

Johnstone, G. (2002) *Restorative Justice: Ideas, Values, Debates*. Cullompton: Willan.

Walklate, S. (2001) *Gender, Crime and Criminal Justice*. Cullompton: Willan.

Index